Villa C

Sally Wragg

Copyright © 2017 by Sally Wragg
Artwork: Paul Burton
All rights reserved.

No part of this book may be used or reproduced in any manner whatsoever without written permission of the author except for brief quotations used for promotion or in reviews. This is a work of fiction, characters, places, and incidents are used fictitiously. Any resemblance to actual persons living or dead, business establishments, events, or locales, is entirely coincidental.

This edition published by Blue Forest Publishing
2017

To Richard, with all my love - and to many more holidays on beautiful Paxos x

And

With special thanks and love, to Matt x

Acknowledgments:

With thanks to Tina and Paul Burton at Blue Forest Publishing for their knowledge and expertise and also for all their help and support during the publishing of this book.

**Also by Sally Wragg, in order:**

Call Home the Heart
The Gypsy's Tale
The Angel and the Sword
Loxley
Nailers' Row & Other Short Stories
Playing for Keeps
Maggie's Girl
Daisy's Girl

# Villa Cassiopeia

# **Chapter One**

Saner people than I would put it down to fate prompting me to turn up at the dentist a full twenty-four hours early. And then, when I escape outside, red-faced and fuming, the sword of Damocles withdrawn - if only temporarily - it's only for the heavens to open, with the kind of drenching rain that sees me yanking up the hood of my anorak and dashing for cover. That I haven't brought an umbrella is a given, my only excuse being, I've had a lot on my mind of late.

Dodging the honking, on-coming stream of traffic, I hurry across the town's main road, instinctively taking refuge in the run-down tea-shop opposite, a higgledy-piggledy premise, used by weary shoppers and shop-workers alike and squashed between Ali's, the Dry Cleaners, and Williams and Son, the Hardware Store. In lieu of a double brandy, tea will have to do.

Scattering rain-drops, tea-cup clutched in hand, I head to the vacant table by the window, and there it is, propped up against the sugar bowl, as if it's awaiting my arrival. A newspaper, folded in such a way, it draws my gaze to the advert it reveals, circled in red biro: - 'Villa Cassiopeia, Paxos. A delightful, bougainvillea-clad holiday home, surrounded by ancient olive groves, sloping gently down to the sea. A stroll from the beach, within walking distance of Gaios. Suitable for a large, happy family. Available to rent due to cancellation, May to August….'

We're half way through May already and our family is anything but happy, so why, rain apart, it strikes such a chord, I've no idea. An obscure Greek island, miles from anywhere and probably as difficult as hell to reach. A squall of spiteful rain dashes against the window. Cold, wet, miserable. It's promising to be a typical British summer, never mind the best part of the day spent dreading a non-existent dental appointment. I'm cold, wet and miserable, too. I read the advert again, taking my time and imagining sky-blue days, folding one into another, presided over by wall-to-wall sunshine and gently shelving olive-groves, rolling down to azure blue seas. Imagine a place like that!

At that moment, a sliver of excitement takes root, a ray of sunshine sifting through the rain-clouds that, metaphorically speaking, generally follow me around. This could be just what our family needs to get it back on its collective feet. Why shouldn't we go on holiday – damn it all, doesn't our family deserve it? Whether we can afford it or not hardly enters the equation, though that perhaps should be my first consideration. An inaccessible Greek island is hardly likely to be cheap and, drop in the financial ocean as it might be to my father, Leon, who has more money than he knows what to do with, I, for one, would certainly struggle to raise the cash. But according to my dear father, who charges through life with all the grace of a bull elephant, I'm impulsive to a fault.

Spirits soaring high above this grubby little tea-shop and already boarding me on a plane to Paxos, I delve amongst the general debris of my bag for my phone and punch in the numbers. There's a pause, a crackle and then, what I should have expected, disappointment, a toneless voice instructing me to leave my name and contact number. Reality strikes. A glance at the headlines of the paper shows what I should have noticed, that it's days old. The offer has probably been snapped up already and answering the advert, no more than giving into a delicious day-dream. Still, I'm nothing if not optimistic. I leave my mobile number and on impulse Father's home number, together with a final and pathetic plea, that my family desperately needs to get away and I'm praying that someone hasn't already got there before us! There's no more to say, and given I've no idea who I'm saying it to, my voice trails away awkwardly. I hate answering machines. I ring off.

The afternoon's wearing on. Chloe will be home from school, full of woe about her last exam, her brother Max, younger by a year and already finished his GCSEs, hot on her heels and demanding what's for tea the moment he throws his hated school-bag through the door. The pair of them trying, without much effort, not to get under Father's feet and grumbling, meanwhile, isn't it about time we returned to Weldon Avenue and the run-down terrace we so lovingly call home?

Are they kidding me?

We're currently living with my father, whose recovery from a minor heart attack is heartening, literally, but has done nothing for his temper or his volatile nature, reminding me of solitary childhood days punctuated by miniature explosions over miniscule matters, none, thankfully, aimed in my direction. At least the football season is over and Daisy, my youngest, aged eight, is with her father until after the weekend. Daisy has had plenty to say about our present living conditions, placing her so far away, a full mile at least, from her many and varied circle of friends. My ears are due a break.

Perhaps I'd better explain… I'm Bryony Dexter, nee Bingham, named by my father after the poet, of whom he is inordinately fond and given, in his cups, to quoting verbatim: - 'What a strange thing man is; and what a stranger thing woman'! I can hear him now, Homberg pushed to the back of his head and underneath which tufts of silver-white hair spring in abandon. His head is thrown back, his thumbs hooked into his braces, whilst he rocks himself back on his heels, pronouncing in mellifluous tones pleasant to the ear but sour thoughts for an elderly solicitor of indeterminate years. After the turbulent years of marriage to my mother, now thank fully severed by decree nisi, it's perfectly understandable. I've had a fairly eventful life, surviving childhood, in the main, thanks to what must have been a benign deity looking kindly upon me. And no doubt this explains why, given my parents' abject example, and desperate for stability in my young life, I sought out and fell in love with one Edward Dexter, dull provincial solicitor in my father's thriving solicitor's firm. Edward, who after marrying and fathering two children with me, shocked everyone, myself included, by running away with the male lead of the local rock band, 'Iron Blessed.' Accepting at last of his true nature, against which he'd fought so valiantly, it says much for the two of us that we've gone on to forge a surprising and genuine friendship, so that towards

Chloe and Max at least, we usually manage to present a united front.

Whilst Edward was finding himself, I, meanwhile, gradually recovering from the explosive ending to my marriage, embarked on a brief and doomed affair with Jake Turnbull, Premiership footballer, now seeking his livelihood in the Championship, and from which liaison, Daisy is the only good to emerge. Perhaps the whole unsavoury incident signified me going off the rails, a belated adolescence I had to get out of my system. But I wouldn't be without Daisy for the world, her presence in it lights up my life, indeed, all our lives, even Father's, whom she deftly hooks round her imperious little finger. But there's no doubting her existence brings with it much baggage, namely my continued association with a man for whom, over the years, I've truly come to despair. Jake is Daisy's father. It's crucial to Daisy's development that the two most important adults in her life enjoy a civilized relationship, at least enough to decide what's best for her. I manage it just but only by suppressing the biggest part of what I'd dearly love to say to him. Wouldn't I! That said, I do like to be fair. One good point in his favour, is that he at least tries to see Daisy on a regular basis - if he's not indulging in one of his many affairs, of which the Sunday papers keeps us suitably and scandalously informed. Indeed, so apt is he at having his name splashed across the front, as well as the back of the tabloids, it's a wonder there aren't a dozen little Daisies dotted around the countryside. The maintenance he pays me is risible but I'll be damned if I'll go cap in hand when only necessity and care for Daisy, forces me to take from him a single penny. He's tight-fisted which is probably why he hangs onto his money, most of which he invests in property and other sensible ventures you wouldn't normally associate with Jake. Was I once truly so naïve? I thought he loved me and that I loved him in return. Reflecting now, I accept I was just lonely and still reeling from Edward.

   Which brings me to the third and final affair of my turbulent thirty-four years, the one with Mikey Witherspoon, a literature student at our local college and would-be writer, several years my junior. It's some months now since 'Bryony's Buffets', my business, 'finger food a speciality', was presented with the task of organizing the catering for the students' yearly bash. The event at which Mikey finally and with the aid of several glasses of cheap plonk, managed to convince me, that the difference in our ages is irrelevant. We have a great sex life but is that enough to base a future upon? Mikey's heavily into classical literature, real ale and rugby, whilst I… Even now, I struggle to know what it is I'm heavily into or even what I want out of life. It's true to say I'm searching for that elusive something, if I've not yet succeeded in finding it. I'd call my tastes eclectic and open to encouragement – an on-going process, I suppose. I come with baggage, of which Mikey is only just becoming aware, namely, a failed marriage, three children by two different fathers, an elderly father with a dodgy heart and a catering business that despite all my striving and willingness to make it work, is slowly sinking into obscurity. Good plain cook that I am, I have to admit defeat to fancy food and vol-au-vents and I'm afraid word has got around. I'm reliable. I'm cheap and cheerful but unfortunately, my culinary efforts never encourage the customers to return for second helpings.

Perhaps some, even all of this, accounts for Mikey's remoteness of late, the cancelled dates, the immersion in his studies, the general feeling my importance in his life is relegated to that of bit-part player. He sees me when it suits him, but not as often as I'd like. Perhaps it's simply that our relationship means more to me than it does to him and it's time I accepted, I'm doomed to live the rest of my life alone.

I mustn't get too maudlin. I need to get home and in the meantime, thankfully, the rain has obligingly reduced itself to a steady drizzle. I depart the tea-shop and relocate the car, a clapped-out, rusty Nissan, overdue an M.O.T. and drive the short distance to Father's. Feeling the first faint prickles of unease, I park up on the gravelled driveway, by the stuccoed porch and hurry through into an ominously quiet house. Earlier this afternoon, I left Father ensconced in the armchair in his study, listening to Beethoven's Sixth, a glass of his favourite malt to hand - medicinal you understand, and strictly rationed since his illness. He isn't in the glasshouses because I go outside and check, nor in the summer house either. Worried, I return inside.

"Father?" My voice echoes eerily around the empty rooms, bringing with it the ominous reminder that today is the second Friday in the month and since time immemorial, the afternoon of the monthly Chambers meeting and that since his illness, my father has been banned from attending. He's not well enough to return to work yet and we had an argument over this very subject at breakfast this morning - the children throwing books into bags and toast and cereal into mouths, me with half a mind on the dentist and the morning I had planned catching up with paperwork and bills, Father's mind, as usual, wholly on himself. He's angling to get back to work, I'm determined he's not ready…

"I'm perfectly well enough!" he exclaimed testily, his face settling into the peevish look I've come to dread.

"Just exercise a little patience, that's all I'm asking…"

We both know patience is a virtue of which he's in desperately short supply. Like father, like daughter, I suppose – so many of my traits, perhaps thankfully, I've inherited from Father. It's why we argue so much. We both want our own way but in this case, I'm determined mine is to be the rule. He slumped back in his chair and foolishly, I took that to mean he'd seen sense.

Faint hope. He's gone to the Chambers meeting. I don't know why I'm so sure of this but I am. Knowing I had a dental appointment, or naturally assuming I had, he must have had it planned and rather than seeing any kind of sense this morning, he was merely biding his time. There's no point trying to reach him on the Smartphone I bought him last Christmas. Father hates modern technology and refuses to use it. I ring Chambers.

"Bingham, Hartley and Pearce?" A pleasant voice answers, laced with a brisk efficiency. It's Penelope, the head clerk, who's been with the firm so long, she knows the partners better than they know themselves.

"Is Father there, Penelope?"

"Ah, Bryony. I was wondering if you might ring. Yes, I'm rather afraid he is…"

"Could I have a word…?" I enquire civilly, between gritted teeth of which we're both aware.

Father's behaviour is no one's fault but his own. He's a law unto himself. There's a pause, the sound of a chair scraped back, footsteps – then shortly, the footsteps returning.

"They've all gone out – I didn't realise he'd gone with them. They must have smuggled him through the back door or I'd have stopped him."

"Don't tell me…"

"A little liquid refreshment. No doubt they thought it would oil the works…"

The up-market wine bar further down the street from Chambers does a pleasant line in single malt.

"Penelope…?"

"Yes, Bryony…?"

"Oh…it doesn't matter…" My voice is filled with disappointment but there's no point taking it out on Penelope, or myself either, for that matter. I only live with Father occasionally, during which times, I do my best to keep him on the straight and narrow. Testy. Irascible. An immoveable force and the only wonder is, by some miracle and dogged determinedness, I've managed to keep him home for so long. If only I could whisk him away to my Greek paradise - neatly solving the problem of his returning to work before he's ready. He won't enjoy the dressing down I'm planning when he gets home, whatever state he's in, I ponder, already beginning to fret over it. Unsurprisingly, I'm the sort of person who searches for solutions before a problem's even half arisen.

Fuming, I inspect the fridge for supper and vent my spleen in chopping onions and garlic, slicing tomatoes, tearing basil into the sauce mixture I stir furiously, wondering the while, if my dearly beloved parent will be sober enough to eat it on his return – if he returns!

The back-door slams. It's Chloe and my mind shifts from father to daughter and how she's fared in her French comprehension, the final exam of her AS levels. Language has never been her strong point but given her lack of revision and the numerous distractions in her life, of which Father is only one, I'm assuming this exam will be pretty much like the rest, in other words, drowned in mediocrity.

I stifle a snort of amusement. Given her obsession with all things Goth, Chloe can hardly be described as your normal teenager, anything but in fact.

She slouches in, five foot four of natural belligerence and hearing Father's words on my lips, a trait, worryingly, I've noticed frequently of late, I squash the impulse to tell her to stand up straight. She's chewing gum. I hate it that she's chewing gum, and whilst I'm about it, I hate it that she's dressed from head to toe in black - high boots, ripped jeans, tailored, velvet jacket, an alarming spiked collar and laced, fingerless gloves. She's dripping with the clunky jewellery she spends her spare time making.

Her beautiful, bright blue eyes are heavily lined with mascara; the whole ensemble plunged into startling relief by garish, bright red lips and nails. It's difficult to find words to describe her hair but it's dyed black and teased into a kind of bird's nest, which is the effect she's after she's assured me and all the rage with the local Goth community, amongst whose number, she's proud to count herself. Her school is modern and progressive or they'd never allow her through the door. She looks anxious and noticing this, as mothers will, tempers my response.

"How did it go?" I enquire, pleasantly.

She shrugs and comes fully into the kitchen to drop her school-bag on the floor.

"Thank God that's over."

Sometimes, communicating with my children is a little like pulling teeth.

"Any tea going, Mum? I'm parched." She fixes me with a smile that doesn't quite reach her eyes and there it is again, that hint of anxiety causing me to multiply it by one hundred. I'm nothing if not persistent. I spell it out.

"I was just wondering how your exam went. You know, the one you sat this afternoon?"

"Does it matter?"

"Of course it matters!" Resisting the urge to shake her, I reach over and pour boiling water onto tea-bags, taking the time meanwhile, to remind myself that though no one would think it, my eldest happens to be one of the brightest girls in the school. The thought restores my equilibrium and I plough on determinedly, "Think of next year when you'll have all the excitement of university to look forward to…

We ought to be looking round at different places though there's no hurry yet. Have you any preferences? Where are your friends thinking of going…?"

Chloe takes the mug I proffer and sips her tea, regarding me pityingly over its rim. "I won't be going anywhere," she says, so matter-of-factly, I could slap her.

"Of course you'll be…"

"I'm not doing my 'A' levels or going onto Uni."

There's a finality in her voice that should warn me.

"I've finished, quit. I've already been into the office to tell them. Crabby old cats – what do they know? Sables' have offered me a permanent job. I'm sure I must have mentioned it, Mum," she finishes, innocently, when she knows full well, she's never uttered a word. Sables is the Goth Boutique in town, where she works on a Saturday.

"Chloe, working Saturday is one thing, you surely can't mean it to be the height and breadth of your ambition?" I say sharply.

I see by her expression that's exactly what she means and I've never heard anything quite so ridiculous in all my life. I open my mouth to tell her so when the door bursts open and Max appears, hurling his satchel under the table and treating me to a glare before stalking upstairs, and all without a word of explanation. The slam of his bedroom door reverberates throughout the house and within seconds, with it, the monotonous beat of his heavy metal guitar. He plays in a rock group which he's formed with his mates from school. He means to be famous or so he tells me and who am I to disagree? There's no accounting for taste.

"Hi, Bro," Chloe mutters, her voice laced with sarcasm.

"You can stop trying to change the subject, young lady…"

"Bryony, thank God! There you are!"

It's Edward, who's followed Max in, his round, good-natured face, spoiled by its uncommon frown, which I take note of but am presently too uptight to trouble over. His arrival is fortuitous. He needs to hear his daughter's plans for her future now, from her own lips and, more importantly, whilst there's chance to argue her out of it. Edward has the happy knack of turning up just when he's needed and because of it, a little of my tension releases.

"I've given Max a lift back from school…"

"Have you? Edward…"

"Bryony…"

"Tell him, tell your father, exactly what you've just told me…" I swing around and frustratingly, find myself talking to empty air, for Chloe has seized her opportunity and slunk away upstairs. Edward's brows draw together in the way, hilariously, I used to find wildly attractive.

"What's up?" he demands, treating me to a closer look and it finally penetrating his consciousness, I have concerns too and for reasons he's yet to discover.

"Chloe's just told me she's not going to University."

"Of course she's going to University…"

"Nor stopping on in the sixth form. She's left school already, apparently. She's going to work at Sables full time."

"I see…"

"I see? Is that all you have to say?"

I glare at this slightly bumbling, rather loveable man, the man to whom I was married for nine long years, years consuming our youth and during which time, in our naive, untutored ways, we did our best to make our marriage work. That we married too young is a plain, unassailable fact and with older, wiser eyes, I accept that now. After the stormy seas of my childhood, ruled over by my mother's bohemian ways, her liking for gin and other, more obnoxious substances over which it's generally best to draw a veil, I was desperate for a long-term relationship to provide me with a stable home life. Father did his best but occupied with running the firm and with the need to keep a roof over our collective heads, Father's best was never quite good enough. Home was chaos, my life was chaos. Thus, I seized on the first likeable man to present himself, who just happened to be Edward. Edward, meanwhile, longing desperately for a chance to prove himself, if only to himself, seized on me as manna from heaven, thinking, by so doing, he could overcome his natural inclinations and only realising too late how impossible that was. We were both trapped, weighed down by the mortgage and the children who so quickly came along, and no matter how we tried, doomed to failure from the start.

I thank God now, despite the shock waves it occasioned at the time, Edward at least had the courage to admit he'd made a mistake. He stands, drumming his fingers on the kitchen table.

Something's bothering him and it's not just Chloe.

"She's talking rubbish, plainly."

"I'm glad you think so."

"Of course I think so…"

"Edward, what's wrong?"

"I'm not sure…"

"Coffee…?"

"Mmm… That would be nice," he murmurs, abstractedly.

I switch the kettle on again, meanwhile shoving the problem of Chloe to one side and busying myself with mugs, milk and coffee, whilst giving him the chance to collect himself. Edward likes to be precise and to tell me his problems exactly so I can give him clear advice. The fact he values my input sums up our relationship. I don't know what he'd do without me – or what I'd do without him, come to that. If only we'd ever been thus!

"Spit it out," I murmur, pouring boiling water onto coffee granules and handing him a mug.

"I've met someone," he says, carefully. He sips his coffee and pulls a face. I make dreadful coffee. It's a family joke.

"And? So what's the problem?"

"It's serious, Bryony. His name's Simon. He's an architect. We're thinking of moving in together."

"Well, that's good, isn't it?" I'm puzzled, not yet understanding. Since his first, heady relationship with Rex Rant, with whom he eloped those years ago, fleeing his marriage and all his commitments,

Edward's engaged in a series of short-term relationships, nothing heavy, no strings attached, re-living his youth I suspect and in the way he should have lived it whilst he was young, if only 'we' hadn't happened. But once or twice recently, I've picked up vibes that he's wanting more – what we had together but with someone he can love properly. In other words, that special man with whom he wants to spend the rest of his life. Exactly my requirements, if such a man exists, I think sourly though I wouldn't admit it, not to anyone – not even to Edward.

"What's the problem? Aren't you sure?"

"I've never been surer of anything in my life."

The deadly seriousness of his tone tells me that from Edward's point of view, Simon is for real. I'm intrigued. Edward's very picky and with standards, virtually impossible to meet.

I sip my coffee. "Then I don't see there's a problem," I tell him, carefully. "If this Simon feels the same about you, and I'm guessing that he does, then go for it…"

"It's partly Max," he returns, startling me. "Max looks like he could be a problem."

"What's Max got to do with it?" I demand. He sounds evasive. Is he picking on Max in a bid to evade other, more difficult issues in this new relationship? He ploughs on determinedly.

"Like just now. In the car. When I tried to tell him about Simon and me and that I'd like them to meet, sometime soon, he nearly bit my head off…"

"Perhaps you caught him at a bad moment. He's had a lot going on of late, Edward, in case you haven't noticed. The stress of living here, with Father and then exams and worrying what he wants to do with his life. He's not exactly academic, is he? He makes out he's not bothered but of course he is. Father couldn't have been ill at a worse time. Besides, Max has always been okay with…well…you know…your…"

"Homosexuality?" he finishes for me. "I always thought…hoped he was. But now, well, to be frank, I'm beginning to wonder."

This doesn't sound like the Max I know and love, the fairest of boys, a boy who always stands up for the minority and the right for people to live their lives exactly as they please. We've always been honest with the children, right from the start, as soon as they were at an age to understand.

"Are you sure you didn't just get the wrong end of the stick?"

"You didn't see the look he gave me."

There could be something in this. I frown thoughtfully.

"He has been behaving oddly of late, I agree. I can hardly get a word out of him nowadays – on the rare occasions he emerges from his room. And talk about falling out with Chloe. It's driving me batty! They're always at each other's throats. I'd put it down to hormones and being at that difficult age but I'm beginning to wonder."

"There's something wrong, Bryony…"

"Whatever it is, it shouldn't be left to fester. It looks like we need to talk seriously to both our children," I conclude, to which Edward agrees.

He goes through into the hall, to the bottom of the stairs and raising his voice above the throb of

Max's guitar-playing, a feat in itself, he bellows for our children to stop what they're doing and to join us – right now! When their father speaks in that tone of voice, both Chloe and Max know to jump to attention. The music stops and shortly, hands stuffed in his pockets, affecting nonchalance, Max clumps downstairs and slouches into the kitchen, shortly followed by Chloe. She looks up for a fight and I'm aware, on the subject of her leaving school without first sitting her 'A' levels, that's exactly what she's going to get.

"Max…Chloe…" I begin brightly.

"What is it? Hurry up, Mother. I'm busy. Band practice tonight," my son drawls, unhelpfully.

"Jeez, here we go again," Chloe mutters under her breath.

At this precise moment, the kitchen door slams back on its hinges and Father staggers in – some entrance and he's chosen his moment. Face glowing, tie awry, hat pushed to the back of his head, the whole effect topped off by the look of angelic benevolence plastered across his face. But that's just it; he is plastered and given his medical condition, that's bordering on the criminal. How could he be so careless with his health! Aware that my temper is on the verge of boiling over, and in the lull during which I consider the right words to adequately vent my spleen, Edward escapes into the hall to answer the phone, which has just started ringing. Its shrill tone shred nerves already stretched to breaking point.

"Father! How could you!" I finally and inadequately explode.

"Bryony, my love…"

He's always been a happy drunk but this time, it doesn't wash.

"Don't you 'my love' me…"

He smiles and hiccups. "Be thou the rainbow in the storms of life," he begins, happily. "The evening beam that smiles the clouds away, and hints tomorrow with prophetic ray…"

Max sniggers. Chloe, more practically and before her grandfather should fall over and hurt himself, pulls out a chair from the kitchen table and helps him into it.

Edward pokes his head around the door and frowns.

"It's for you, Bryony," he says. "I can't make head nor tail of it. Some chap about a villa, somewhere I didn't quite catch. He says to tell you the summer tenancy's yours, if you want it. I suspect it's a wrong number but it's rather a bad line, I'm afraid…"

# Chapter Two

A sleek, slim-lined jewel of the ocean. Spumes of sparkling white foam leap up as the ferryboat Christa, pride of the Ionian Sea, sets off from Corfu, heading speedily away from the port into the bay. Since we disembarked from the airport-taxi onto the port, the sea has grown choppy and the cloud above it thickened, the speed with which we've been hustled aboard this luxury ferry leaving me to suspect, if we're not to be delayed, time is of the essence. Storms are an occupational hazard in this part of the world and blow up out of nothing. A little like the Greek temperament, I muse, leading me to the following thought that I should fit in here without difficulty.

Only the solid heat we encountered earlier this afternoon when we emerged, tired and dishevelled, from the plane at Corfu airport, reminds me in any way, we've just endured a four-hour flight from a grey and wet East Midlands. I can't believe we're here, zipping effortlessly across the Ionian Sea and that in the space of a few short days, I've organised not only myself but the rest of the family, on this so unexpected adventure together. Daisy apart, whose joyous prattle signifies her approval of our plans, I'm aware no one else in the party is quite so appreciative of my efforts. I've booked a holiday, out of the blue and for want of anything better to do with their collective time, my family has condescended to join me. Begrudging about sums up their general attitude.

I've parked myself on one of the benches open to the elements, at the stern of the boat and across from Father, who is sitting with his back against the rail, staring gloomily over my head to Corfu, fast disappearing into the distance. It's too late to back out now and I can see he's wondering if it would be worth his while to dive overboard and swim ashore whilst there's still time. Thankfully, common sense prevails. He's exchanged his homburg for a panama and despite the sour expression beneath it, it lends him a jaunty air, his only concession to the unassailable truth that from this point onwards, this family is officially on holiday. His feet are splayed, his rugged head thrust forward, enabling him to rest his chin on his hands, presently folded over the Malacca cane he's taken to using of late and the only indication of his illness. Daisy's chatter washes harmlessly over him, a constant drip, drip of her stream of consciousness which can drive you mad, if you allow it. Her shrill voice, filled with excitement, raises smiles of amusement amongst our fellow travellers, who don't have to live with it. Italian and German tourists mostly, together with a smattering of Greeks, returning from the day's work on Corfu.

Despite the informality of golf shirt and slacks, what he considers appropriate holiday wear, Edward, the other side of Daisy, is too quiet, and I can't help thinking, he's troubling about more than Max's resentment over Simon. Simon's due to fly out and join us in a couple of days, the soonest he could arrange time off from his busy architect's business and thus giving Edward time to get to the heart of what's bothering Max. Hopefully, in the relaxed atmosphere of our holiday, our son will bring himself to confide in his father. Max isn't himself, I admit and even the prospect of this holiday has failed to return him to his usual cheerful self, nor encourage him to open up to me or even to Chloe, charmingly unfazed by her father's love life.

"Goths are outcasts from society," she told me earlier, on the plane coming over here. "We appreciate that everyone is different and has their own individual perspectives and concerns…"

"Are you trying to say I don't understand my own family?" I protested, at once.

Her shoulders lifted disdainfully. "All I'm saying is, we're sensitive to other people's needs. It's all a matter of respect. We're deeper into society than anyone else and we don't judge."

"You mean I do?"

"I don't mean anything."

Of course she meant plenty but despite the low opinion she obviously has of me, I consider everything she outlined, an admirable creed to live her life by and it's reassuring to know we have so much in common. She's gone to sit with Max, slouching in the cabin area, as far away from his embarrassing family as possible. Father says it's his age and he'll grow out of it and I pray he's right.

Greeks, it appears, aren't yet ready for a Goth invasion and Chloe's progress through the boat has turned heads, even though, as token to this holiday, she's tuned down her ensemble, replacing ripped jeans and clumpy boots with pin-striped pants and high heel shoes in which she struggles to walk. Her tee-shirt is ripped, hanging tastefully off-shoulder and emblazoned with a picture of Siouxie and the Banshees, a group popular amongst the Goth fraternity. Should I say something? Is it worth another argument? I have enough on worrying over this holiday I've so impulsively embarked us upon. But, summing up, I can't help thinking I've done right. Our family needs time away right now, removing Father neatly from the temptation of returning to work before he's well enough and giving Edward and I time with our children, of whom I include Daisy.

Unbelievably and acting upon yet another of the impulses to which I'm increasingly prone, I've sold 'Bryony's Buffets' as a going concern and if I've had to borrow the money from Father to tide us over, once the sale has been completed, it will pay for our share of this holiday and even better, leave me with a small sum over for our return. I don't want to think about that yet. The transaction's in the hands of the firm's solicitors, leaving me with nothing to worry over other than what to do with the rest of my life. I'm sorry to see the business go but better to sell up before it drags me under with it. I have a horror of debt and I'd never live off Father. Perhaps he'll conjure up an opening in Chambers. He's hinted as much, heaven forbid, the last place I see myself.

I'm missing Mikey already but I'll have to get used to that, given that on a tentative enquiry if he'd care to join us on this jaunt, he blithely informed me, he already has plans for the summer, mainly a walking holiday in Switzerland with a party of fellow students, rather hinting at the fact our relationship has meandered on to its natural conclusion. Given our disparate ages and tastes, it's hardly surprising and sadly, it appears that Mikey and I are not to be. 'C'est la vie' as they say. I don't know the Greek for this, which reminds me…

Delving into my bag, I locate the Greek phrase book, an impulse buy from the airport, and for once ignoring the needs of my family, I spend the rest of the journey happily teaching myself a few useful phrases. 'Hello' and 'thank you' and 'how much is that?' kind of thing, soon discovering, that if fascinating, even ordinary words become incomprehensible and unpronounceable when translated into Greek.

My lips move silently, as if in prayer.

"Land! Land!" Daisy shrieks, recalling me to my senses with a start.

I don't know what I'm expecting. Easily as excited as Daisy, I twist round to see a sloping mound of green, rising gently up, out of the water, fair maiden of azure-blue seas, a mass of olive and cypress trees, dotted with match-stick villas, painted in golds and yellows and ochres so I wonder happily, which one might be ours. The fruition of days of hectic organisation, times I thought we'd never get here and that the whole idea of us coming away together, as one big, happy family, was patently ridiculous.

Carried away by the palpable hum of excitement amongst our fellow travellers, even Father perks up. He pats Daisy's head and then beckons through to Chloe and Max to come and join us. Edward, he ignores and has done for the whole journey I realise, the thought temporarily denting my exuberance and reminding me of the state of uneasy truce, constantly threatening to erupt into full-scale war, that exists between the father and grandfather of my children. They tolerate each other, I like to think for my sake, though that's doubtfully so. They've come on this holiday together but not without a deal of negotiating on my behalf. Not only did Edward have the temerity to desert Father's cherished only child and for reasons with which he struggles to come to terms, but worse, he left to set up a rival business in Derby, taking with him too many of the firm's best clients. Given the hot-bed of gossip around Chambers at the time, he could hardly have done anything else but that's not to say, I can't see it from Father's point of view. He trusted Edward and given my lack of interest in the family business, after all, his pride and joy, once Edward married into the family, Father had naturally envisaged that once he himself retired, Edward would step neatly into his shoes. Father never troubles to keep his opinions to himself and though for Chloe and Max's sake, he puts up with Edward's continued presence in our lives, left to his own devices and without the children, his grandchildren, to trouble over, I know for sure, he'd want nothing more to do with him.

  The port rises serenely into view, a bare, tarmaced area through which clumps of straggly grasses grow and beyond it, backed against a wall, a bar, shaded by a garish awning and under which are several dilapidated deck-chairs. The Christa's arrival occasions much activity and, as if by magic, the dock is suddenly full of people and cars and a cacophony of shouting and hooting. The Christa hoots back. We heave too and one of the crew jumps down and fastens the gangplank, at which point, there's a mass exodus of passengers, amongst which our little party is swept along, into the crowd milling on the quayside, waiting for bags and cases to be rescued from the hold.

Heat and noise and the first, fat drops of rain from a dark and angry-looking cloud overhead that's followed us all the way from Corfu. This isn't rain as we know it in England, I quickly discover. Nothing I've experienced so far is at all like England. It dries as it hits the ground, filling the air with a steamy warmth. Regardless, chattering cheerfully in incomprehensible Greek, tossing cases and bags, one to the other, with practised ease, the crew carry on unloading and somehow, in all the mayhem, passengers are connected with luggage, with hired cars and waiting taxis, manned by excitable Greeks. With a shriek of metal, two cars crash into each other, causing even more excitement and shouting, though other than the vehicles' two drivers, no one seems remotely concerned. The more seasoned travellers, meanwhile, trundle away on foot, dragging their cases behind them and I look after them longingly. Eventually and rather worryingly, only our party remains and as the rain is falling for real now, we take refuge in the bar. Father sits on top of the packing cases, looking forlornly out to sea, where the Christa rocks gently, as if she's fallen to sleep.

"I presume we are to be met?" he complains, testily.

"So I was told…" I reply, thinking hurriedly back to the conversation I had, several days before, with the man in the Greek booking office, the bored voice speaking in a pigeon English I struggled to understand, so I emerged from the call not sure what I'd arranged and with only the vaguest idea that the journey would unfold one way or another. Journeys generally do, though I've had my fair share of mishaps over the years. "Perhaps our villa's within walking distance," I suggest, tentatively and looking fruitlessly around the deserted quayside for someone to ask. Everyone's gone and the truth is, I have no idea of the exact location of our villa nor, indeed, how far it is from this port. I pray that it won't be too far or too much of a strain for Father, who is fortunately looking in the rudest of health.

"I could take a stroll into Gaius and see if I can drum up transport," Edward suggests helpfully. Gaius is the capital of the island and only a short distance away. So much we know. Father mops his brow with his hanky and snorts. Max sighs pointedly and despite her peaceful Goth intentions, Chloe looks ready to explode.

At that moment, the sound of rain pattering against the awning is broken by the steady clip-clop of hooves. Turning onto the tarmac from the road above it, is a large, fat, grey donkey, pulling a cart. A hunched figure, wearing a bright-red mackintosh and hat, presently pulled down low against the rain, sits in the driving seat. Incongruously, and as if in defiance of the weather, the donkey's comically elongated ears, two flattened stalks which twitch like antennae, emerge from a battered straw boater from which the rain drips. It comes to a halt in front of us and the figure jumps down, revealing it to be one of those women whose age is impossible to guess and in any case is an irrelevance. Her gaze sweeps confidently over us before coming to rest on Father. Instantly, her whole demeanour brightens.

"Villa Cassiopeia?" she enquires, in a deep, husky voice.

"That's us!" I exclaim, taking charge. "We're waiting for our taxi…"

She raises one well-plucked eyebrow. An interesting face, older than I thought and full of character, I sum up, as is my want, often wrongly, I admit. But it's a lived-in face, with a disconcerting habit of staring straight through you, I find, as reluctantly, she tears her gaze from Father and turns the blaze of her attention on me. She sweeps one heavily be-ringed hand towards the cart.

"Here is taxi! I take you to Cassiopeia – yes?"

As a form of transport, it's hardly what we expected but it seems churlish to refuse. Besides, there's no alternative. Seeing Father on the verge of one of his more acerbic put-downs, I take his arm and yank him from his seat, just as, at that precise moment, a streak of lightning flashes across the sky, hotly followed by a rumble of thunder and then another, even louder. It decides us. The awning is scanty and it would be dangerous to stay here. Besides, we're getting wet.

Whilst we load our luggage and climb aboard the cart, directed by our driver to pull up the extending tarpaulin roof over our heads, kept folded at the back and which should give us at least some kind of shelter, she introduces herself.

"My name is Agatha Giannopoulus," she informs us, once she's settled into the driving seat. She turns back towards us.

"Pleased to make your acquaintance," I return, politely and then make my own hasty introductions, including all our party. Apparently in the mood for conversation, she smiles graciously.

"Island's taxi-service is no good, too many tourists," she explains. "I help out. Tourists like donkey cart and like Boadicea, the donkey. Boadicea, she good girl – sometimes!"

On such short acquaintance, I don't dare to disagree. Displaying a worrying number of tombstone teeth, Boadicea folds back her ears and brays. We're a heavy load for a single donkey, even one as large and fat as this one, but she's stronger than she looks and when Agatha points a whip in her general direction, she trundles off happily enough. Agatha is native to the island she tells us, in her unconventional English, twisting round from her lofty perch to impart the news, whilst simultaneously fixing Father with a flirtatious gaze. There's no need to worry. Father is an old hand with frisky clients. Notwithstanding, she flutters her eye-lids and tells us, and Father in particular, that her husband was a bad man, a wastrel who spent his life in drink and in alternating spells in the jail on Corfu – and better that he ran away and deserted her, than she should spend her life with such a man, she exhorts us, heatedly. Surprised as we are to be regaled with such personal information on such slight acquaintance, it's all very interesting and helps to while away our journey.

The rain is falling in earnest now, dashing onto the roof of our carriage, covering the world in a misty grey and obscuring the view ahead, so I change my mind about how different everywhere is here, in

Paxos, and think instead, how much this looks exactly like England. But we've surely never come this far to endure even more rain and misery! The truth that we have, settles on our party like a shroud, lowering our collective mood. I'm glad when Agatha turns back to concentrate on the road ahead, for the ride is a bumpy one, taking us along narrow, pot-holed roads with extreme corners and giving glance, here and there of turbulent seas below, filled with high waves which hurl themselves spitefully against the jagged rocks which line the coastline. Every so often, as we progress, mostly uphill, I'm aware of the carriage wheels, uncomfortably close to an increasingly vertiginous drop into the valley below.

Noticeably paler, his knuckles showing white, Edward hangs onto the side of the cart. I can't stand heights either and it's with a general relief when our transport finally departs the road and turns us off onto a beaten track, obscured by over-hanging branches. The slight lifting of our spirits is tempered with the growing realisation, we've only exchanged one set of tricky terrain for another, this one full of twists and turns between ancient olive groves, surrounded by stone walls, in various states of disrepair, some tumbling down and blocking our path so circumnavigating them becomes increasingly difficult. With a surprising delicacy, Boadicea picks up her hooves and threads a path daintily between them. Here and there, we pass a pastel-lemon or rose-tinted villa, peering shyly from masses of greenery, until I begin to wonder, what exactly is this place and where is our destination's end – indeed if it will end or if this isn't some fool's escapade upon which I've brought us. I daren't tell Father, on the strength of a description I read in the paper, I've taken our accommodation on trust.

At last, in the middle of nowhere in particular, Agatha pulls the cart to a halt and climbs down, turning quickly to help us disembark. As we stand around awkwardly, hunched against the rain and wondering what comes next, she lugs the cases from the back of the cart and piles them up around our feet. We're too wet and miserable to help her. She's done with us. Rain drips off Father's hat and I can hardly bring myself to look at the scowl beneath it. He takes out his hanky and mops his face then firmly and pointedly, he takes hold of Daisy's hand. Even Daisy is subdued and I can only think it's all my fault. What have I brought us to? No-one says it, but I know that's what they're thinking.

Sensing an air of constraint between what, after all in other circumstances, would be a happy holiday party, Agatha sweeps one hand towards a pair of high, wrought-iron gates behind us and the sight of which I've so far failed to register. This, she informs us, helpfully, leads to Villa Cassiopeia. Disconcertingly, the smile slides from her face and she shakes her head at us, as if, in some way and for some unknown reason, she's sorry for this place to which she's brought us. Her duty towards us apparently completed, with a speed belying her age, she jumps back up onto the cart and with a hurried wave in our general direction, turns donkey and cart neatly around before rattling quickly off, back the way she's come. The sound of carriage wheels dwindles and fades into the distance. Only the rain remains, and olives trees. So many olive trees.

"Oh, God," Father moans.

Edward wasn't married to me those long years without being aware of Father's temper. Throwing me a look of solidarity, he picks up a case, in either hand, and makes determinedly for the gates. Max has got there before him, turning the iron handles with which the gates are adorned, and heaving them open. They're in need of oil and creak theatrically.

Disparate thoughts sift through my mind. We're tired and wet and I'm filled with trepidation. I've no idea how this holiday will work out with our family so at loggerheads. Father so awkward, casting daggers at Edward at every opportunity, Chloe and I at boiling point over this business with school, and not forgetting Max. I can't work out what's bothering Max and this is beginning to worry me. The tension between us is palpable and Edward doing his best to engage our son in a matey dialogue is only making matters worse. Throw in the weather, which we appear to have brought with us from England and the fact I've never yet seen this place, not even a picture, to anyone of saner disposition, our problems could appear insurmountable. Why didn't I ask the booking office to email me views before I booked?

My impulsiveness will get me into trouble one day. I think it already has.

Heads bowed against the sheeting, stinging rain, we make our way along a gravel path, flanked either side by the inevitable olive-trees, emerging abruptly onto the lower section of a two-tiered, stone terrace and from which vantage point, I receive my first sighting of Cassiopeia.

My eyes lift and widen in surprise. Our villa has presence, is my first thought, surprised by it and an atmosphere hanging over it, like a shroud, which catches my breath. I was meant to come here, I think next, though I've no idea why I think it. Beyond my gaze, lies an incredibly ancient, three-storied, not quite square-shaped house, with a sloping dusky-red roof. A pile of gently mouldering stone of differing subtle hues and colours, ranging from cream to delicate rose-pink, in the Venetian style I've read is so common to these parts. Even in these wretched conditions, that it has unassailable charm is plain to see. The shutters, with their flaking green paintwork are closed, giving the impression of the house gently slumbering. The bougainvillea I've been so looking forward to seeing, turns out to be a single vine of indeterminate age, presently rattling against the upper shutters, a splash of pink and lilac-purple against its mass of greenery.

Mercifully, despite the weather, the front door is propped open and after ascending the stone steps onto the second terrace, we reach it thankfully. Sanctuary. It's a relief to get inside, out of the rain and into the dim, white-washed hall in which we find ourselves. There's a door facing us, either side of which stand wicker chairs. The floor is flag, the area by the front door, sheeted with rain. To one side are railed stairs, leading both upwards to the bedrooms and downwards, to the kitchen, I presume. On the adjacent wall is another door, leading through into the interior of the villa and to the side of which stands a vase holding fresh flowers, which emit a faint aroma of summer, battling against what I realise, is a worrying smell of damp.

Automatically, I reach for the light switch by the side of the door, alarmed when I switch on and off, several times and nothing happens. A flash of lightening quickly followed by a crack of thunder makes me jump and in the brief light it provides, illumes Father's face. He looks on the point of apoplexy.

"Oh, that's just great," Max observes, trooping in behind me.

"It's probably just a power cut. Must be the weather…"

"You hope…" This from Chloe.

Where's their sense of adventure? Edward braves the rain to fetch the rest of the cases and cursing audibly under his breath, Father disappears downstairs to locate any possible candles before it gets too dark to see. We've had nothing to eat since the airport lounge, hours before the flight.

Leaving him to his search and with Daisy excitedly leading the way, the rest of us troop upstairs to explore. Doors crash back, shutters are flung open, letting in the damp, dwindling light to the dusty corners of each room. On the top floor and in the largest of the front bedrooms, we come to a halt, entranced by sight of the rain-soaked garden beneath, and there, beyond it, to a mass of olive and cypress trees with wildly waving foliage and over the tops of which, we see, in the far distance, the vast expanse of shimmering, opaque light that is the sea. A living, breathing, moving entity. Even now, even weary as I am after all our travels, it has the power to lift my spirits. We're here, and no matter how inclement the weather, there is the sea, a mystical beast to a lady of indeterminate age, from the land-locked Midlands. It's not just the sea, it's this villa, too, I realise. A house filled with mystery, I feel it in my bones and already, I'm intrigued by its history. Who owns it and why don't they live here? Why can't I shake off this feeling that in some way, destiny has prompted us to rent it? If I owned it, I'd never let it out to strangers.

The rooms are sparsely furnished, each with requisite number of cupboards, drawers and beds at the bottom of which an unknown hand has left clean sheets and blankets, neatly folded. Leaving Chloe, Max and Daisy inevitably falling out over who is to have which room, I return downstairs to the kitchen, to a flickering, dancing light and to Edward, setting the last of several candles into its saucer. Candles are dotted about the room.

"Alright, my love?"

"Do you know, I rather think I am!"

Unaccountably, my spirits are soaring. We're here and this holiday will be what we make of it. The children clatter back downstairs, gravitating by instinct towards the kitchen, as Father emerges from what has proved to be the cellar, where he has discovered buried treasure.

"Wine cellar's well-stocked," he observes, humour thoroughly restored and happily depositing two dusty bottles of red wine on the long, deal table.

I'm not sure we ought to help ourselves but I'm easily persuaded, I rattle drawers and cupboards and find a bottle opener and glasses. The kitchen is a dark, subterranean cave, deep in the bowels of this house and yet I sense that already we've discovered the house's heart and that in days gone by, people were once happy here.

Pans and saucepans, and strings of dried herbs and onions, hang on the wall, beside a dresser with rustic-style crockery, a little chipped but functional, I discover, on further inspection. Its presence is overshadowed by a vast and complex black-lead range, with which at some point, I will have to get to grips. I'm filled with unexpected confidence. As a sop to modernity, in one corner, there's a standing fridge which, if nothing else, at least suggests the present power cut is of a temporary nature. Even better, it's stocked with essentials, milk, juice, cheese and butter, tomatoes and olives and thick, creamy Greek yoghurt. The bread I discover on top, wrapped in a cloth, is proper Greek bread and further proof of human hand at work. By its side, is a pot of local honey.

As the rain lashes down outside, rattling at the windows and tiles and with the wind whipping the branches of the trees into a frenzy, we sit cosily around the table to supper, our faces illuminated by candle-light, for once a family at ease with itself. It won't last, I know so much and it's merely that everyone's too tired to argue. This so unexpected calm in the tempest of our lives has sprung out of nowhere and I wish it was always thus.

Daisy is drooping with tiredness. After we've eaten, despite her protestations to the contrary, she lays her head on the table and instantly falls asleep. I take a candle and go upstairs to make her bed, shortly followed by Edward who carries her up in his arms.

Rocked to sleep by a mixture of exhaustion and excitement, she hardly stirs. She's never stepped foot out of England before. I could never afford it and I've always had too much pride to ask her father to finance a trip. Poor Daisy, shunted between two warring parents, one of whom has more money than sense and thinks only of himself.

Edward stands at the bottom of the bed, staring down at her thoughtfully.

"Don't you wish she was ours, Bryony?" he asks.

"You think we haven't enough problems with the terrible twins?"

His smile at this quip fails to hide his sadness.

"What is it, Edward?" I ask. "Problems on the Simon front?"

I've hit the spot exactly. "I'm the rebound from a bad relationship," he begins. "It's shattered Simon's trust, unfortunately and he doesn't feel able to make a commitment yet. I'm afraid, he's hedging his bets. He thinks we should give each other space."

It sounds so much like Mikey and I, only pride prevents me from telling him so. It hurts too much to talk about me and Mikey yet, though when I am ready to talk, it will be to Edward, to whom I can pretty much tell anything. When you consider all we've been through, the unhappy years of marriage, the trying vainly to fit together lives that wouldn't fit, that's nothing short of miraculous.

We've moved to the window and are talking in whispers.

"Simon sounds a pretty sensible, together sort of guy?" I prompt.

Edward stares balefully through the rain-dashed window, to the garden beyond, now shrouded in darkness. There's a distant murmur of the sea and the wind battering against the eaves so that again, I feel the strangeness of this place.

"He doesn't love me like I love him," he admits, carefully.

"Perhaps he just can't show it."

"I wish that was all it was."

"And yet you want him to meet the children?" I gently prompt.

He shakes his head sorrowfully. "That was just wishful thinking on my part, I expect. But what can I do now it's planned?"

He can't do anything and there's no answer to this. I'm too sensitive to point out, in any relationship, there's always one partner does most of the loving whilst the other is content to receive. I wouldn't hurt Edward's feelings for the world. He's right about the children though.

"You can't really blame him, Edward," I hazard, cautiously. "To lead you on and then let you down once you were both committed, wouldn't be fair – on either of you."

Edward winces at the truth of this whilst I, realising what I've just said, feel the heat warming my cheeks, for that's exactly what Edward did to me, who had no inkling of his true nature, so carefully concealed, he scarcely acknowledged it himself. His elopement shocked everyone, even in Chambers, where given the juicier details confided by their clients, at the best of times are a pretty tolerant and broad-minded lot. Bitter experience has taught me we can never truly know another person. Edward's saving grace is that my behaviour at the time, hadn't much to say for itself either. Pushing him into marriage because I wanted a home and a family, a sanctuary from life occasioned by my wayward upbringing. We were young and we didn't know how to handle the situation, that's our only excuse. But I would have been content for our marriage to have gone on forever and it wasn't until it fell to pieces that I discovered Edward was not, and never has been, the love of my life. That man I've yet to meet and I'm beginning to wonder if he even exists.

"We must be grateful for what we have," I murmur, struggling for the right words, a difficulty at the best of times. Edward's hand finds mine and closes around it.

The house is beginning to work its magic already because we stand together like this for long, contented moments, happy in each other's company and without the need for words.

# **Chapter Three**

A pale light awakens me and I stretch lazily, blinking and yawning like a contented cat. My head sinks back into the pillows, my gaze drawn to the window and sight of the cloudless sky beyond, sun-bleached to the palest blue I've ever seen. I've not felt so relaxed in a long while. Too long, I think, happily, and that this holiday is my most wonderful idea ever, leaving my problems belonging to someone else, not me, a person too far away to trouble me.

But there's more jolting at my consciousness. The rest of the house is up and about and I'm the only one still lounging in bed, so unusual an occurrence as to be unthinkable. But the sound of Chloe and Max arguing and Daisy's prattling observations as to who has said what and to whom, drifts through my window, the whole mixed in with Edward yelling for quiet and amazingly, Father singing, a lullaby, I vaguely remember from my childhood. They could be up to anything, I muse, a worrying thought seeing me leaping hurriedly out of bed, to pull on shorts and tee-shirt from my case, still to be unpacked. I was too tired last night, flaked out, in fact.

Despite my haste, I'm drawn to the window with its spectacular views and I take a moment to fling the shutters wide, standing to pull a brush through my hair and breathing in deeply, such a benign, calm atmosphere, I think I must have died and gone to heaven.

It's true. I haven't imagined it. Beyond the trees, lies the sea, shimmering and sparkling in the sun, the sight mixing headily with the sound of birds, chirruping and trilling from the branches of the olives and the cicadas singing in the garden below. A scent of flowers assails me and of spices and of warmth, only increasing my sense of well-being.

Reluctantly, I tear myself away and go downstairs, heading quickly for the kitchen, my good mood only slightly diminished by sight of Father, at the stove, which in my absence, has miraculously been coaxed into life. He's frying eggs and in lieu of an apron, has a tea-towel tucked into the waistband of his trousers. It's like walking into an oven.

"Morning, my love. Edward and I have the stove going, as you see…" he informs me loftily, waving the spatula in my general direction and splattering fat and grease in wild abandon. Leaving aside the perplexing problem of how my Father and ex-husband have managed to work at anything together, without one wanting to murder the other within five minutes, it raises the question of by how long I've overslept.

The electricity's back on and miracle of miracles, Father has discovered an ancient toaster, a steadily growing pile of toast on the table bearing testament to the fact. He ladles eggs onto plates, then bellows deafeningly for the children, who appear from the direction of the garden, a tousled Edward in tow, who grins at me sleepily.

By the door, an unknown hand has left a basket of oranges and we supplement our scratch meal with freshly squeezed orange juice and honey and yoghurt, which we carry outside, sitting to breakfast at a table on the terrace, complete with stunning views.

"A meal fit for a King," I murmur, happily and yet unable to help glancing anxiously around the table. No one argues and that's another miracle though of course, it doesn't last.

"Or Queen," Max chips in spitefully, looking straight at Edward and receiving a kick under the table from Chloe for his pains.

Bad as he's been of late, this isn't like Max.

Rising above the jibe, Edwards seizes his chance to make connection with his son. "I thought I'd go into Gaius this morning to see about a hire car," he says, through a mouthful of toast. "Why don't you come, too, Max? We can have a root around, see what's what, make a morning of it if you'd like?"

"And I was hoping you'd come with me, Chloe?" I jump in, heading her off, just as she's about to suggest she joins them. "See what the local shop has on offer. You can come with us, Daisy…"

The mutinous look settling on my little girl's face should warn me. Bang goes Edward's idea of spending time alone with Max. Out comes her bottom lip. She won't help us and wild horses won't force her to change her mind. I can't begin to think where she's got her stubbornness from. Her father, I shouldn't wonder.

"I'm going with Edward and Max," she states, imperiously, brooking no argument though I do my best.

"Come on, love, be fair…"

"Want to go…"

"Darling, you'll only slow them up. It's too far for your little legs…"

"Oh, pleeese, Edward, pleeeese say I can come too…"

Edward has no defence against it.

"Oh, I don't see why not," he returns lamely, the look of resignation accompanying his words reminding me of his lack of backbone, a contentious issue throughout our married life. Father snorts in disapproval and rising from the table, retreats to a chair on the lower terrace with his book. That, it appears, is how he means to spend his morning and after the strenuous effort of getting him here, I'm pleased, for once, he's being so sensible. There's also the small matter of the third bottle of wine he fetched up from the cellar last night but we won't go there. I didn't drink it and neither did Edward, as far as I know but the bottle is still empty. I throw him an exasperated glance.

Shortly, Edward sets off with Max, an over-excited Daisy in tow, whilst Chloe and I veer off in the opposite direction, towards what we presume is the nearest village, one of the many with which the island is dotted. Small clusters of habitations, held together by church and local shop. The sun is already climbing high in the sky, bathing the world in a golden light so that I think, amazed by it, the difference with which sunshine makes us view the world. Gone is the dreary grey greeting our arrival here. The world is washed clean, turning our path from an obstacle course, sent by unkind hand to torture weary travellers, to a windy little track, bestrewn with tumbling flowers of varying hues and colours, set against a backdrop of olive groves behind which the sea glimmers and winks, as if determined to accompany us on our walk.

Even Chloe is impressed, though she won't admit it and especially not to me. Her dark-purple tee-shirt is ripped and hung with chains and I can't help wishing she hadn't plastered her face with quite so much make-up, perversely hiding the natural beauty she has in abundance, inherited from her mother's side, of course. She's young, she'll learn, or at least, I hope she will. I recognise it for what it is, a defence mechanism, an act of defiance and a statement to the world in general and to me in particular, that she'd rather be back home in Derbyshire with her Goth friends than here, in Paxos, with me. I want to talk to her about school and university but I daren't broach the subject. Our relationship has hit a rocky patch and I'm praying that this holiday will put it right.

"Any plans for the day?" I ask, tentatively.

Her shoulders lift into a moody shrug. "There's nothing to do here, is there."

It's not a question. She's made her mind up already. I plough on despite it. "It says in my guide book, Gaius is a great place, full of shops and tavernas and day-trippers from Corfu. You're bound to meet people there of your own age…"

"Hah…"

"Chloe, I do wish you'd at least try to meet me half way…" I snap, breaking off as our progress is halted by any number of hens, squabbling and clucking their way across our path, like a mother's meeting, all heading towards the shade of a nearby olive grove. They don't seem to belong to anyone, only to themselves, I think, my burst of ill humour immediately forgotten. The sight makes us both smile, our delight deepening when shortly, their progress is followed by a gaudy cockerel who struts haughtily after them, only to be greeted by his harem, when he arrives, with a vague indifference.

He flies off, nettled and sits sulking on a tree stump.

"Sorry, mum…" Chloe volunteers, unexpectedly. "I'll try and do better, I promise."

From her, this is progress indeed. Heartened by it, I even try out some of my newly acquired Greek on one of the locals we happen to pass, an elderly man in dirty blue overalls, mending one of the broken walls, of which there's an abundance.

"Yassou," I murmur, politely.

He stops his work and looks up. "Ah, English," he returns, pityingly and rising to his feet, chuckles quietly to himself. "You…on holiday?" he asks, inquisitively. "You like Paxos, yes..?"

I can't help smiling back. "It's beautiful and as for all this sunshine… It's doing us the world of good already, I can tell you. We're staying at Villa Cassiopeia," I finish, struggling for anything else to say to him, yet hardly prepared for the effect of my words, for no sooner are they out of my mouth than his smile vanishes and he crosses himself. Then, without another word, he abandons his work and hurries quickly away, towards what I presume to be his home, a faded, sandstone villa, peeping out between the solid leaves of a huge, cactus-like plant. Chloe frowns and stares after him.

"How rude."

"I wonder what's got into him…?"

"It was when you mentioned the villa, Mum…"

I think she's right but I haven't the slightest idea why mention of Cassiopeia should bring about such an odd response. It's very strange but given we can't chase after him and demand to know what's wrong, we refuse to let the incident spoil what is turning out to be a remarkably happy day.

Resolutely, we carry on to the end of the track, a five-minute walk at most and at which point we re-join the main road and progress to the brow of the hill, to the village, only a short distance away. That's rather a grand title for what is, after all, merely a cluster of tiny, pastel-shaded houses, in varying states of disrepair. There's also a church with a bell-tower and a solemn little graveyard, across from which is a sprawling taverna, from the roof of which drips a vine with huge, saucer-shaped blue flowers. From someone's front window, a tiny bread shop operates and next to this, narrow steps lead down to a general store. The sight of a donkey tethered outside, wearing a straw-boater, should have warned us.

"Boadicea!" Chloe cries in delight.

She brays peevishly at the sight of us though condescends to let Chloe stroke her muzzle, without making too much fuss. Inside, another surprise is waiting for serving behind the counter is Agatha, a woman with fingers in many pies it appears. As we dip our heads and enter the shop's low doorway, she beams happily and throws her arms wide.

"Is good, yes? Please, have good look around."

I don't need further encouragement. An old-fashioned shop like my mother used to talk about and I can't help but be delighted, like stepping back in time. Packets of pasta and rice, tubs of olives and tins of goods with odd Greek names, alongside open sacks of sugar, coffee, beans and cereals, all vying for space with trays of potatoes, carrots, tomatoes and onions and oddly shaped lettuce. There's a fridge full of cheeses, yoghurts and beers and on a small wooden table besides it, a wicker basket in which nestles small, prettily-coloured eggs, collected from the hens we passed on our way over here, I suspect. I hardly know where to start. Happily, I grab a basket and without even trying, quickly fill it. Agatha stands, arms folded, watching me with an acquisitive eye and nodding in satisfaction as a second basket fills, equally as quickly.

"Agatha, who is the old man who lives in the sandstone villa, the one with a large cactus-looking plant outside it? He was repairing the wall," I tell her, impulsively, meanwhile trying to decide between baskets of dusky-rose peaches and sun-filled, golden apricots, then greedily filling paper bags with both. I heave the first basket onto the counter and make a start on unloading. "He spoke English, well, as a matter of fact..." I finish off, not even sure this passes for a description. All these islanders speak English so well.

"Is Spiro? White hair...wears blue overalls?"
"That sounds like him..."
"Ah, Spiros...is good man..."

It's difficult to explain but at least I have to try. My brows crease with the effort of putting what I want to say into words that Agatha can understand. Outside, Boadicea snorts in frustration. She, at least, understands.

"He was perfectly pleasant until I mentioned Cassiopeia…"

"Ah…"

"It appeared to upset him in some way. He ran off… I can't describe it in any other way. It all seemed rather strange…" I finish and already sensing a certain wariness of expression in Agatha's demeanour. I'm recollecting now, too late, how oddly she behaved, when she dropped us off at the villa yesterday, a day that seems a lifetime ago, now. Time, I realise, has lost all sense of meaning and I take it as a sign this holiday is doing us good and that already, we're beginning to relax. Agatha carries on running my goods through an antiquated till but her cheeks have flushed up.

"Is old man…old men have strange…how you say…fancies…" she murmurs though I have no clear idea what she means. I plunge on bravely.

"Agatha…what is it about Cassiopeia, exactly? It's almost as if this Spiro was suggesting there's something wrong with the place…?"

"Is sad house," she volunteers unexpectedly, confusingly when we've settled in so happily.

"In what way, sad?"

Her hand flaps vaguely and her shoulders lift into a shrug of dismissal. I'm to get no other explanation, at least one that makes any sense.

"Not sad now though…now you have come…you and your happy family," she answers quickly as if she's sorry for telling me even so little.

"How the heck are we to carry this lot back?" Chloe chips in, bored already and eyeing with alarm, the number of bags around our feet. Seizing on the distraction, Agatha calls through a doorway behind the counter.

"Milo… Milo!"

A young man appears, laying the book he's been reading open on the counter. There's enough resemblance between the pair to tell me that this is Agatha's son. The same direct gaze and self-satisfied air, as if no matter what life throws at them, they'll never be fazed. I wish they'd teach me the trick. Agatha gazes at him adoringly and I'm remembering now, all I've read about how important families are to the Greeks, as my family is to me, too, I realise, with a little rush of affection for Chloe, whose boredom has miraculously vanished along with Milo's appearance. With his olive complexion and dark, wavy hair, he's very good looking. His gaze widens as he catches sight of her and instantly, his lips widen into a lop-sided grin he takes no trouble to hide. Even I have to acknowledge how strange Chloe must appear to anyone not au fait with Goth culture. Instantly, her shy smile of greeting vanishes, too quickly replaced by the scowl over which I've often had cause to despair.

"Milo will take shopping on bike," Agatha informs us, firmly and apparently blithely unaware of the atmosphere which has unexpectedly infiltrated her happy little shop. She beams dotingly as Milo tears his gaze away from Chloe and quickly gathering the numerous bags of shopping together, disappears outside. Shortly we hear the sound of a scooter revving, the favourite form of transport for young people on Paxos, I've learned. Chloe's ill-humour emanates towards us in waves.

"We'd better get back," I mutter, hastily, filing the matter of Spiro's behaviour to the back of my mind, to be taken out and examined later. We pay the bill, which, considering all we've bought, is surprisingly little, say our goodbyes to Agatha and to Boadicea and then, footloose and fancy free, we dawdle back along the windy track, arriving at our villa just as Milo is setting off back to the shop, having left our bags in a shady spot on the top terrace. A thoughtful boy, I conclude and hardly deserving of the look Chloe treats him too as, smiling and waving cheerfully, he re-passes us on his scooter. Chloe is not one to forget a slight, real or imagined, and sadly I sense a promising friendship stifled at birth. And when a little light holiday romance might just have been what was needed to put her in a better frame of mind! Father appears from inside, as a car door slams and from around the far side of the villa, Edward reappears. Worryingly, he's alone.

"I've left Max and Daisy having a browse round the shops," he informs me quickly and only too aware of my propensity to make a catastrophe out of a minor occurrence. "The car's organised. We thought we'd have lunch out. I've popped back to fetch you both and Father, too, of course," he concludes hastily, as if suddenly aware of Father glowering across the terrace. It's a great idea and typical of a man who desires above all things, to please.

"You all go…" I urge.

"But why don't you come, too, Bryony? It would save you cooking, if nothing else…"

I've no intention of bearing the burden of the holiday catering alone. My family would never survive. "Or you," I tell him, sternly.

"Or me…" he concurs, sheepishly.

I flap my hand vaguely, in the direction of the shopping. "This lot needs unpacking and besides, it'll give me chance to get my bearings…" Which is all very true, and a tactful way, for me, of saying, after all the work of getting my family here, what I crave most, is time alone. Surprisingly, Father concurs with the plan, a willingness that should set alarm bells ringing but only occasions a vague sense of disquiet I quickly dismiss. He's adult and compos mentis, after a fashion. It's about time I started to trust him again.

And thus, matters are satisfactorily arranged. Edward, Father and Chloe pile into the car, a Renault of dubious origin and colour, whilst I lug the shopping into the kitchen and make a start on the unpacking, arranging fruit tastefully in bowls, packing the fridge and cupboards with enough food to last us through a siege, and that done to my satisfaction, going upstairs to unpack my belongings. Finally, reckoning I've deserved it and not wishing to raid the cellar further, I uncork one of the bottles of wine we've bought from Agatha's, wandering out onto the terrace to drink it, drawn by the sound of the sea, and the strongest of feelings that I must make the most of this holiday, for who knows what life will hold once we return to England? England, which seems so far away, an uninhabitable life on a strange planet, peopled by aliens.

Already, Paxos is working its magic, unknotting knots, calming my soul and putting the world to rights. The gentle, mesmeric pulse of waves rising above the olive trees is the most wonderful sound in the world to me. There's something else too, disturbing the calm of my equanimity and which at first I struggle to decipher, a steady clink-clink, as of a spade turning over soil, coming from beyond the trees in front of the lower terrace.

Curiosity roused, swallowing the last of my wine, I slip gratefully into the shadow of those ancient trees and make my way towards it. I haven't had chance, so far, to explore beyond their boundary, assuming, wrongly it appears, that they merely carry on unhindered, down to the sea. Thus, the clearing I come upon, so unexpectedly, pulls me up sharply.

Before me is a thriving vegetable plot and it's as if I'd wandered back home again. No less than an allotment, its plants cultivated into neat rows by a loving, green-fingered hand, all old favourites, beans, cabbages, lettuce, cucumber, tomatoes, the latter grown in glass houses in England of course and nothing at all like these fine specimens. Butterflies hover, a fluttering, golden cloud and in their midst, toiling over a hoe, is a man, his battered straw hat pulled low over his face so at first, I can't decide what to make of him.

He's seen me for he straightens up, pushing his hat to the back of his head with a gnarled thumb, revealing his thin-featured, sun-burned face, a man past middle-age, who might have sprung from the earth over which he's toiling, his eyes shades of blue, like the sea and flecked with ocean-green. He doesn't speak. He might be mute, or there again, not altogether there, though he looks bright enough for that's a keen intelligence shining from those strangely reflective eyes.

"What a beautiful garden…" I begin, hopefully, my smile fading when my words elicit no response. He knows no English whilst I, the interloper and most to blame, know so little Greek.

For long moments, we stare at each other, no way through the language barrier and neither of us with any idea of how to progress. Such is life and there's little I can do, though I feel there ought to be something. I don't feel put out. His manner's difficult to explain but he has a presence about him that's oddly comforting, if that doesn't sound too strange.

A man, tending his garden. What's not to like? It reminds me of home, but in a good way, miraculously excluding my problems there. I wonder if this plot belongs to the villa but I hardly like to ask. From the little while I've been here, I've discovered already that Paxos knows no boundaries where properties are concerned, a hotpotch of pastel shaded villas, one blending into another so effortlessly, it's difficult to know where one property ends and another begins. It only adds to the island's quaintness and already I'm growing to love it.

I'm doing little good here, I decide. I say goodbye politely, in English, unsurprised when, other than a dip of his head, I receive no response. I walk on calmly, away from the villa and making instinctively for the sea, glimmering and shimmering in the bay below me, as if it draws me by a thread, caught up in the region of my heart.

Past yet more olives, I emerge onto a gravel path between cypress trees, which leads me on to yet another rough track, this one meandering off at a tangent to hug the hillside. It leads me sharply down to the sea, to a shingle beach, upon which the sea hurls itself, before pulling back, with a sharp hiss, to regroup and repeat the process, endlessly, on and on, leaving me so mesmerized, I can only stand and stare.

The place is deserted and it's with difficulty that I tear myself away and find somewhere to sit, propping my back against a rock and staring out seawards, taking such delight in the simple pleasure, that I can think of no place else I'd rather be. England has worn me out, I realise abruptly, with father's illness, with my failing business and perhaps most of all, in my failing relationship with Mikey, which has upset me more than I've cared to admit.

At which thought my eyes grow heavy and…

I have no idea how long I've slept but the sun is sinking low in the sky, a golden orb, reflected in the still, calm sea, edged with shafts of shifting, liquid gold. Everyone will think me lost, or worse, that I've been captured by pirates and thrown overboard, fodder for hungry sharks. I hurry away from the beach, making my way quickly back up the path between the trees, past the now deserted vegetable plot and through the olives to the villa, only to discover, annoyingly, when I arrive there, so hot and out of breath, the villa is deserted and the travellers have yet to return.

I've no idea what might have kept them but imagining they'll have worked up fresh appetites, I make a start on supper, deciding after re-inspecting the fridge, on a simple egg salad. I'm tired. They'll be tired too and all we'll need is simple, plain food to replenish our energy levels. After it, I plan on nothing more strenuous than a date with my book and an early night. As a family, we've never eaten early, preferring instead to sit around the table together, late evening, discussing the day's events. It's easier to keep tabs on Chloe and Max that way and it never seems as if I'm prying, even if I am. But as the afternoon slips effortlessly into evening, I start to worry. I mean, solitude's fine and I've enjoyed my time alone but now I'd appreciate a little company, even that occasioned by the mixed bag that is my family.

    I try to phone Edward but Edward has his phone turned off and only a major catastrophe would ever make me think of phoning Chloe or Max. I haven't quite reached that point yet and I'm left with nothing to do but wait. I've set the table out on the terrace and I wander moodily outside, only to wander back in again, standing to drum my fingers on the kitchen table and starting to worry all over again. Where can they be? Edward is an impatient driver at the best of times and unused to both the car and driving on the opposite side of the road, roads moreover in a bad state of repair and filled with pot-holes. What if they've met with a truck, a lorry even, on a bend, high up in the hills? At once, my head is filled with sirens and flashing lights, ambulances and hospitals, the Greek policeman at the door and kindly neighbours offering condolences and strange food I'd never be able to eat, nor even understand a word they say to me...

At that moment, with a whooshing sense of relief, I hear a car engine and doors slamming and then, and this slightly lowering my spirits, I hear Father, the pitch of his voice suggesting to me, who's heard it so often, that he's not quite himself, in fact, impossible as the idea initially is to me, that he's had too much to drink. He can't be drunk of course, not again and not after the doctors' repeated warnings. But when has Father ever taken notice of doctors? Edward is bound to have stopped him from drinking too much, I reassure myself. Dear, kind, dependable Edward, who would never dream of bringing his ex-father-in-law home in such a state, when trusted to look after him…

The party descends the stairs into the kitchen, a procession of guilt if ever I've seen one, with Father bringing up the rear, his face as rosy as a fire-cracker. He beams at me happily. My spirits plummet, the results of his transgressions undeniable.

"How much have you had?" I ask, acidly.

"A mere glass of ouzo, my love…"

"Hah!"

A crafty gleam comes into his eye. "Man, being reasonable, must get drunk…"

"Must he indeed…"

"The best of life is but intoxication…"

"Edward, this is all your fault!" I snap, rounding on my unfortunate ex. Max laughs nastily and I glare at him whilst Chloe, ever the diplomat and quickly summing up the situation, grabs Daisy's hand and hustles her back up the stairs. She's right; Daisy has no business seeing her grandfather in such a state, nor her mother governed by uncontrollable temper. Edward is mortified.

"Bryn, I'm sorry but I couldn't stop him. He went off with a Greek family he got chatting too and never bothered to tell us. We couldn't find him. It's why we're so late…"

"How could you!" I screech, like any common fishwife but having to offload my temper somewhere, it just so happening to be poor Edward upon whom it's turned. Even more unfortunately, just at that moment, there's a knock at the kitchen door, which is standing wide open. Through a red mist, I see a man, standing awkwardly on the doorstep, looking in and appearing embarrassed, as well he might, given the scene he's most likely witnessed.

"Simon! You're early – but what a wonderful surprise!" Edward cries, his voice echoing with relief.

He hurries towards him and embraces him heartily. Gently disengaging himself, Simon enters the kitchen, dropping his case thankfully at his feet.

"I managed to cancel appointments and catch an earlier plane. You must be Bryony. I hope I haven't put you out," he says, smiling towards me and holding out his hand.

What a waste to womankind is my very first thought. As if in a daze, I take his hand, trying to ignore my heart, doing a double somersault, as everything else, even Father's drunken behaviour, flies from my head and I find myself looking at the most incredibly, drop-dead, gorgeous-looking man, I've ever seen in my life.

# Chapter Four

I haven't imagined it. When I pass the pot of honey to Simon at breakfast, my hand touches his and I snatch it away as if I've been scalded. My gaze is drawn to his. A Greek God and I wonder however dull, provincial Edward has managed to snare him, though of course, I wouldn't dream of breathing a word of this to Edward. This morning, Simon's in full holiday mode, turning up to breakfast in shorts and a tee-shirt, high-lighting his toned, muscular frame. Looks aren't everything and I always go by personality first but all the same…

No wonder Edward's fallen for him, him and half of Derbyshire, I shouldn't wonder.

We're breakfasting on the terrace, sitting around the table, en famille, even Father, if still pale from yesterday and with a headache to match. Serve him right, too, I think, taking my attention from Simon long enough to thump a cup of coffee in front of him. He winces but he's asked for it. What kind of an example is this to set the children, his grandchildren, after all, little as he thinks of their respective fathers?

"Sorrow is knowledge," he murmurs pathetically, taking a couple of headache pills from the box on the table beside him and washing them down with the coffee. He pulls a face. Paxos, it appears, has done nothing for my coffee-making.

"Are you alright, Bryony?" Edward asks, anxiously.

"It's not me you should be asking," I snap, spitefully, unable to help it though what kind of impression I'm giving Simon, I dread to think.

"We've all been there," Edward replies, ever the diplomat.

"You bet," Simon chips in, catching my eye.

He doesn't have to try hard. Colour floods my face though I'm aware that he's merely being grown-up and polite. I'm his hostess and considering I was once Edward's wife, he's not quite sure yet how to be with me, or how I'll be with him, come to that. Let's face it, it's a difficult situation and some women wouldn't even countenance it, never mind one behaving like a love-sick teenager.

I'm old enough to know better and I hide my confusion buttering toast and drinking coffee, which is piping hot and burns my mouth. Anything but look at this gorgeous hunk of a man sitting across from me. He's gay and happens to be the love of my ex-husband's life. I'm patently out of order harbouring any kind of feelings towards him and besides, even if he had the slightest suspicion the way my thoughts are running, he'd obviously run a country mile.

Edward clears his throat, as if what he has to say next is important. Edward doesn't deal in trivialities and whatever he says should always be treated with respect.

"We thought we'd take a trip into Lakka today and go for a walk round the harbour to watch the boats come in. Why don't we all go, take a picnic and make a day of it? We could fit into the car at a push…" he suggests. Lakka is the little port lying at the head of a bay, on the north coast, only a few miles drive away, within walking distance even, for those with energy enough. The trip's obviously taken on importance because it's a chance for Edward to introduce Simon to his children, of whom he includes Daisy.

After his confidences of yesterday, I wonder how things are between them. Simon appears perfectly happy but I can't help noticing Edward seems on edge. In respect of Father's feelings, Simon made up his bed in a spare room last night. Can I read anything into that? It's none of my business, whatever the cause but that doesn't stop me wondering how Edward feels about it.

"I want to go to Lakka!" Daisy cries, clapping her hands.

"Count me in," Chloe agrees, surprisingly, so surprisingly, I throw her a troubled glance. But she's bored and a trip out might be just what she needs to shake her back to normality – or whatever passes for normality in Chloe's world.

Max bites into a slice of toast.

"How about it, Max?" I ask, tentatively. He's hardly spoken a word to Simon since he arrived, nor to his father, come to that.

"How about what?" he asks, deliberately provocative.

"How about going into Lakka with Dad?"

"I've plans."

"What exactly?"

"Just plans."

"It doesn't matter," Edward chips in, placidly but obviously hurt. "We can go another day…"

"No, you must go," I insist, prompted to it by Daisy's little face which instantly crumples in disappointment. Why should she miss out because of her big brother's obstinacy?

"You'll come too, Bryn?" Edward asks, brightening at once.

I shake my head, my eyes sliding towards Father, who sits, eyes closed and with his head, rested in his hand. Ouzo obviously doesn't agree with him or at least, the amount of ouzo he put away yesterday. I'm thinking back to my childhood and wondering if he's always drunk too much and it's just that I've never noticed before. Is it a problem? Do I need to talk him through it, arrange counselling or something? My head full of all the ghastly accoutrements accompanying life with an alcoholic, my gaze slides back to Edward who, sensitive as ever, has cottoned on to my line of thought.

"We can go another day. I don't like to leave you here on your own…"

"I'm hardly alone when there's Max and Dad. Please, you go and when you come back you can tell us all about it. I promise I'll be along on the next trip…" I murmur quickly and to prevent further argument, springing up to make a start on stacking the pots. In any case, I want to have a look around Gaius today and the walk will do me good.

"Here, let me do the pots. You made breakfast remember," Simon offers helpfully, the perfect guest. He jumps up and relieves me of the plates. Simultaneously, in the branches of the olive tree overhanging the terrace, a bird begins to sing, romantic, soulful stuff, like angel's song – or is that just in my head? Simon is over six foot and he's standing so close, he's invading my space. I feel like a giddy teenager again, a time I can just about remember, my current anxieties making just about as much sense to my muddled way of thinking. I have to place myself out of danger and sooner rather than later.

    I smile, a shaky, sickly smile, turn on my heels and flee.

    I can't imagine Simon has any idea of the effect he has on me. For heaven's sake, why would he! He's just being polite and I find myself hoping, desperately and not just for my sake, that his relationship with Edward works out.

    My gaze slides to Max, plodding alongside me, still surprised that when I suggested a walk into Gaius, he agreed to accompany me. We've left Father reading on the terrace and have set off before it gets too hot, planning on returning in time to prepare our invalid some lunch. I've no intention of allowing this holiday to pass us by and in any case, I shall have to devise some exercise, if only to control my weight with all this delicious food I'm eating.

    But as we walk, given the problems the day has brought already, entirely unexpectedly, happiness envelops me. We're here, in beautiful Paxos, where sweetly scented flowers mark our path, pointing the way to olive groves shelving down towards the gently lapping sea, like music to my unaccustomed ears. Max has hardly spoken and only then in monosyllables. Resisting the urge to shake him, I move the conversation on to other matters.

"Isn't it wonderfully peaceful here?" I gush.
"Suppose…"

"I mean, how could you not be happy in a place like this?"

His shrug suggests he could, very easily.

"I'm glad I managed to sell my business before I left England, at any rate. It's something less to worry about," I carry on hastily, trying a change of subject, all to no avail. Max can't contain his indifference.

"Really…?"

"Yes… Really. Though I'm sorry I won't be able to pass it over to you when you're old enough, which I've always wanted to do. Did I ever tell you that was what I had in mind? If you ever had a fancy for catering, of course. Though I don't suppose you've had much chance to think about that yet, have you, or what you want to do when you leave school?"

With Max, further education appears out of the question and given how difficult this conversation is already, I daren't even suggest it. Unforgivably, I'm babbling and I don't need my son's pained expression to tell me so. Boys are naturally reticent and Max is worse than most.

"I hate school. I can't wait to leave."

"Darling, I'm sure it can't be that bad…"

"It is, believe me…"

"I'm sorry…" I conclude lamely, inadequately and wishing now I'd never raised the subject.

We've reached Gaius where we dawdle along the curved waterfront to the town's main square, captivated by sight of the gaily coloured houses marking its path and where already, early tourists are claiming their favourite tables and calling waiters for tea and coffee. Now we're here, I take the opportunity to do a little shopping, meandering with Max along the delightfully narrow, cobbled streets leading off from the square, lined with market stalls and antiquated shops, full of bric-a-brac and soaps and olive oils.

I'm chatting away, an up-to-the-moment commentary on all I see, prompted to it by the cacophony of sound and colour around me, the hotchpotch of sensation that I'm discovering makes up Gaius life, hardly expecting a response but then realising, shamingly and all at once, Max is nowhere in sight. Here one minute, gone the next, blast the boy. No wonder I've been getting so many strange looks!

Five minutes frantic searching and then, as if instinct leads me there, through the dusty window of a little back street antique shop, full of gently mouldering furniture, I see him. I press my nose up against the window and peer inside, seeing immediately what's brought him here. Besides a grandfather clock with a cracked face and resting against a carved wooden chest, is a battered guitar. I watch as Max picks it up, with such a reverence and intensity of expression, I've no need for anyone to tell me how much he's missed playing. A mother should know these things. So why don't I? He loves music and he loves the group he's created with his school mates. Of course, he must be missing it when by rights, if only I hadn't dragged him out here on a whim, he would be back home, playing the gigs he had lined up. Gone is the surly, indifferent youth I've sadly become too used to, replaced by a young man full of life and charm, chatting animatedly to the proprietor who, expecting a sale, stands by rubbing his hands.

Resting his foot on a chair, Max settles the guitar against his knee and plays a few chords. He seems to like what he hears because he plays them through again. I can hear the melody he's picked out, through the open doorway and one or two other passers-by stop to listen too. But then, abruptly, as I watch, the smile slides from my son's face and reluctantly, he puts the guitar down. I know instantly what the problem is because, other than the little money I provide him with, which slips through his hands like grease, he has no money and if I hadn't been so tied up with Mikey and losing my business and then with Chloe and the stupid argument over school, I might have paid more attention to this fact.

Bad parenting on my behalf. I closed my ears to what I considered to be a painful noise instead of encouraging his obvious talent. I can't afford it but… Hey, what's that to do with anything? It's never stopped me before! What is money if not to spend, even money I don't have, at least not until the sale of the business goes through.

I open the door and slip inside and even before Max looks up and sees me, I've caught the shop-keeper's eye.

He's a boy transformed, the old Max I've not seen in a very long while. He looks down lovingly at the guitar, now propped up against the café table and I can see already how much his fingers are itching to

71

play it. Before we tackle the walk home, we sit, drinking coffee, watching the swallows ducking and diving over the bay, their shrill, piping call a musical accompaniment to our conversation.

"Are you sure, Mum? I can't believe what you've paid for it…"

"I was wondering about taking it back…"

He realises that I'm joking and his face lights up.

"Thank you," he says, humbly. "Thank you so much…"

"You'll have to play something for your dad…"

I'm watching him over the rim of my cup so instantly, I'm aware of the shadow crossing his face at even the mention of Edward, the cause of which, I've yet to discover. It's about time we tackled the subject of his recent behaviour and there'll never be a better opportunity.

"Max, what's wrong?" I ask.

Instantly our camaraderie has gone, evaporated as if it's never existed.

"Nothing – everything's just terrific!" he snaps back.

"Are you worried about your exam results?" This is the obvious scenario and I can't help wondering now, why I haven't asked him this already. He shakes his head.

"Why should I worry? Straight Cs and Ds, that's me. That's what I'm expecting and that's precisely what I'll get. Besides, I can't be bothered with all that rubbish stuff…"

I complain at this. "Max, your attitude might be a bit better. Goodness knows what your dad would say if he could hear you…"

"Hah! Dad!"

"Yes, Dad – and that's just your reaction every time his name's mentioned. What's happened? You two used to get on so well. Is it because of Simon – you're feeling pushed out because of Simon? You do know how important he is to your dad?"

Clumsy as ever, I'm bombarding him with questions, too much, too soon.

"I don't even know the bloke," he answers, sulkily.

"That's why Dad has asked him along on this holiday," I tell him, patiently, if wondering why I need to repeat the fact. "It's a chance for you, Chloe and Simon to get to know each other, I mean really get to know each other, Max. The trip to Lakka is a case in point. Dad's hurt you didn't want to go along."

"If I'd gone, you'd never have bought me this guitar," he answers, craftily.

"Max, you have to try."

He shrugs and looks away, shutting me out, except I'm not about to let that happen, especially now we've come so far. "Have you some kind of a problem with Dad – about him being gay, I mean?" I demand and in the way I'm past master of, instantly making a difficult situation infinitely worse. But it's what I've been thinking and chip off the old block as I am, I've always believed in plain speaking.

"Of course I haven't a problem with that…"

"Straight or gay…there's no rights or wrongs. It's just the way some people are."

"He shouldn't have married you."

"Max, that's none of your business…"

"I don't see why!" He's raised his voice and an elderly Greek lady on the table to our left, turns her head to stare. He has the grace to blush. "Sorry…I'm sorry," he continues, wretchedly. And then he stops, staring at me long moments so that I see he wants to say more but it's difficult and he doesn't even know where to start.

"You do know you can tell me anything?" I prompt.

"What if I'm…like that, too…?" he asks, quietly.

Is he confessing he's gay? Like most mothers, I've imagined the scenario but never really thought it through. "Would it matter if you were?" I ask him, meanwhile, asking myself the same question, too. I know at once it would matter, difficult as that is to admit. I don't want his life cluttered with the difficulties that being gay would bring.

"The lads at school say like father, like son. They're always saying it. They won't listen."

"I see. So that's it." I pick up my cup and take a gulp of coffee. He's been bullied at school and he's never said a word. No wonder he hates the place! Edward bottles things up, too, so I suppose in one respect, those boys are right, it is like father like son. My heart fills with anger at what he must have gone through. "If that's what they're saying, Max, deliberately, to hurt you, take no notice. They'll get fed up. Bullies usually do."

He sips his coke, absorbing what I've said and wondering if he has the strength to act on it.

"It doesn't matter to me whether you are or not." I prompt.

A wry amusement springs into his eyes. "I'm not, okay?"

"Okay…"

"So you've no need to worry on that score."

Relief rushes through me. "I wasn't worried. Well… Only a little," I confess. "But on the subject of your dad…. None of this happens to be his fault."

"No… I can see that."

"So cut him some slack."

He frowns at this, taking it as criticism, which it is but then, thankfully, his expression clears. "I'll try," he says. I can't ask for more than that. But is it really so simple that he's only been blaming Edward because of his difficulties at school? There must be more to it but at least we've made a start on untangling this mess we've got ourselves into. I'm not used to solving problems. Problems arise and generally hang around for ever, is my experience of life.

Simultaneously, we've both become aware of the waitress, hovering by our table, a pretty, attractive young girl with a sense of life about her, I see that Max has noticed too.

"You play?" she asks him, looking at the guitar and speaking in the broken English everyone on this island seems to speak. Instantly, Max's face lights up. Shyly, he picks the instrument up and strums a few notes and then begins to play, a piece I've never heard before so I wonder if it's his own composition. I do know he writes music, if only because Chloe has told me so. He writes for the band but I sense it's not this kind of music, so gentle and lilting, so ideal for here and now and for such a place, full of a swirling emotion, expressive of its composer.

The café's gone quiet and people walking past on the waterfront, stop and listen too. When he stops, finally, thinking he's made a spectacle of himself, a spontaneous applause breaks out.

"Is beautiful…" the girl says, leaving me with the impression she doesn't mean the music.

Max is blushing now and seeing that we've finished our drinks and that he's descended into dumb inarticulacy, I say goodbye for the both of us and hustle us out onto the quay. I've embarrassed him, for he hates this kind of personal stuff. He's embarrassed even walking alongside of me. Mothers are uncool, I have no illusions concerning teenage boys, nor girls, either, I muse, thinking of Chloe. My attention is diverted by a rack of English papers hanging up outside a gift shop, a closer of inspection of which reveals them as yesterday's papers, the headline on one of the better-known tabloids causing me to stop and take a second look. 'Turnbull does a runner. Rovers deny rift…'

What the hell's Jake been up to now? Pulling the paper from the rack, I read the article through rapidly which, old news or not, doesn't make for pleasant reading: -

'Sources at Burleigh Rovers suggest that their mercurial centre-forward, Jake Turnbull, has failed to turn up for pre-season training, for which transgression, his club, whilst denying a rift, have slammed him with a fine of two weeks' wages. Little enough for a player of Turnbull's wealth and standing but bound to have further inflamed a volatile situation. This isn't the first time in Turnbull's chequered career he's been at odds with his club. No one appears to know the player's whereabouts, though club sources point to problems in his personal life and rumours of late-night drinking sessions, as a reason why he might be lying low…'

"What's up now?" Max reads the article over my shoulder and snorts in disbelief.

"Just Jake, in trouble again," I mutter between clenched teeth, my first thought being for Daisy and what a dead-weight for a father she has, my second, the happy coincidence that I've so conveniently whisked her out of the country. My little girl is at an age where she questions everything and she doesn't need this complication in her life. I enter the shop and pay for the paper, stuffing it hastily into my bag to read through later.

"What a prick," Max says, summing Jake up succinctly and in the way only he can.

I can't disagree. He slings his guitar over his back and we walk on amiably, talking of this and that, anything but Jake and meanwhile inspecting the vessels moored along the waterfront, a pleasant mixture of fishing boats and shiny, brand new yachts.

We wander past gnarled old fishermen, sitting on low stools on the quay-side, mending their nets and who greet us with a friendly 'yassou'. Finally, we reach the port and 'The Christa' bobbing sleepily on the water, where we turn off, onto the road, to begin the steep ascent back to Cassiopeia. A place, I realise, with an unexpected rush of affection, I'm already beginning to think of as home. Just then, we hear the steady clip-clop of hooves and turn to see Agatha, bowling along the road behind us. Boadicea brays in recognition.

"You want lift?" Agatha demands, drawing the cart alongside.

It seems rude to refuse and I'm grateful in any case. It's hot and sweaty and I'm too used to England, where the seasons blend into long months of cold and wet. This heat is burning me up. It's wonderful to climb up onto the cart, next to Agatha, sitting atop a still, fresh world. Max makes himself comfy on a sack of grain in the back and we continue on our journey. I can see he's itching to play his guitar and shortly, unsurprisingly, a gentle melody accompanies our progress, of which Agatha appears appreciative. She turns around, throwing him a smile of encouragement.

"Is good boy," she says. "You come, play at Milo's party tomorrow? Is birthday party…"

Max stops playing. "I dunno…" he begins, then stops and colours up, thinking, rightly, he's been rude. "I mean, thanks but…"

Agatha's smile widens. "Please come…and bring Chloe, too?" She glances at me to check she has the name right, though given her obvious antipathy to Milo, quite what Chloe will think of the invitation, I dread to think. "You enjoy. Party good fun…all of you come…" she orders, expansively.

"Father too, I hope?"

There's no mistaking the sparkle in her eyes at the mention of Father but there's no way we can refuse her. The matter apparently settled to her satisfaction, Agatha concentrates her attentions on the steep curve of the road ahead. The cart rattles over pot-holes and loose stone and shingle and I cling on tightly, squeezing my eyes shut and thus avoiding sight of the steep drop into the valley below, my mind's eye meanwhile, seeing mangled bodies and Father left to Chloe's not so tender mercies. It would at least concentrate his granddaughter's mind, I muse, a little sourly. But gradually, the sound of Max's playing relaxes me and common sense prevails – such a talented boy! My eyes snap wide. This is too good an opportunity.

"You'll be used to holiday-makers staying at Cassiopeia, Agatha," I begin, hesitantly and shooting her a sideways glance. "But you must just get to know them when they have to go away again..." I grind to a halt, surprised the shutters don't slam shut at this inquisitiveness.

"You first visitors at Cassiopeia for…two years," Agatha returns, matter-of-factly and wonderfully, appearing in the mood to talk. Having imagined we were merely the next in line of a steady stream of visitors, I'm surprised at this information. But who's been looking after the villa, mean-time, I wonder? Direct questioning appears the best way forward.

"The house is usually empty then?

Head tilted thoughtfully to one side, like a small, plump bird, Agatha considers the question.

"Sometimes, one, two bookings a year. Sometimes none for two year and place is empty…"

She's surprised me again and set me wondering afresh about this villa of ours. It is rather odd and surely, she must see it, too?

"But it's to the owner's advantage to let it, surely?"

"Of course…"

"I expect he stays there himself – or herself, whoever she is!" I smile, satisfied I've reached the truth of the situation but Agatha only shakes her head.

"No-one knows owner. House is bought and sold and is all I know. Sometime people stay, sometime not. Is looked after by…how you say…caretaker…Tomas. He looks after house and garden, too."

It seems a strange set up. "The old man I've seen working in the vegetable patch?" I ask.

"Patch?"

"Garden, I mean…"

"Ah, is Tomas, yes."

It's as I thought, the garden does belong to the villa. I take my time assimilating this information.

"Does Tomas live in the village? Doesn't he know who employs him? Why doesn't he?" I demand, questions springing so quickly into my mind they tumble out, one over another. Agatha frowns.

"Booking office pay Tomas' money into post office. That's all he cares…"

"Oh, I see…" I say, though I don't, not really.

"Tomas live in village," she agrees, patiently. "Before Tomas, for long, long time, there Theo and Anna. Before that, Eleni Mitsopoulos but she old woman now and lives with daughter, on Corfu. She worked for family who once own Cassiopeia…" She sighs heavily and shakes her head and I can't help thinking, there's so much more she could tell me, if only she'd care to. I'm intrigued, longing to know more but sensing I've asked Agatha more than enough.

"What family did this Eleni worked for, Agatha…?"

"Ah, just family..."

There it is again, that air of disapproval, as of shutters closing, giving the impression there's trouble associated with Cassiopeia which shouldn't be talked about.

"Agatha, what is it about Cassiopeia?" I burst out, impatiently.

Perhaps I've offended her. Probably it's only that I've allowed my curiosity to run away with itself and she's simply had enough. "Is sad house," is all she says, only re-iterating what she's said before when we broached the subject. Her lips clamp tightly and disapprovingly shut. The villa doesn't make me sad, on the contrary, I've never felt so happy in a very long time but perhaps that's just getting away from England, with all its consequent problems. Bright blue skies and sunshine go a long way, even post-Mikey.

Suddenly, I'm thinking of Simon and guiltily, I do my best to banish him from my mind. Hunky, gorgeous Simon. The last thing I need is to start fantasizing over him but out here, in all this heat, it's hard not to let thoughts stray. We've reached the turning off the road and I've already decided, to save Agatha, that's as far as we go.

Despite her protestations, we climb down from the cart, standing to watch, as turning to wave cheerfully, she carries on to the village to her shop, presided over in her absence by Milo, she's told me, her voice full of pride. She loves her son, as I love mine and it's a bond between us, I recognise. Two single women, doing the best we can, if sometimes, despite all our efforts, our best never quite being enough. Nothing is ever enough but that's just life and I accept it as such.

"What's up, mother," Max asks, ever sensitive to my mood.

I'm not sure myself and I shake my head. I've no idea what's troubling me, only that there's some mystery attached to our villa which, one way or another, I'm determined to discover. A holiday project if you like.

Back home, I send Max off to enquire the progress of Father's hangover, whilst I return inside, into the cool and welcoming depths of our villa, going straight upstairs to my room and the view from its open window.

The sound of the waves rolls towards me, shifting and swelling onto the shore below, a rhythmic pulse that has already found its way into my heart. It calms me, helping to dispel my tiredness. Who once owned this house? Who owns it now? And what is it to do with me in any case! Agatha doesn't know or perhaps, for reasons of her own, it's just that she won't tell me. It shouldn't matter when we're here on holiday but my curiosity is stirred and in a way that makes me determined to see it satisfied.

And as I watch, Tomas, as I now know him, appears from the direction of the village, disappearing quickly into the shade of the olive trees and out of sight, hurrying to work in his garden, I presume. A solitary man, at one with this island which has a vibrant life of its own and of which I'm only just becoming aware. I remember the basket of oranges left at the door and the welcome the house provided on our arrival, the food and the wine and the fresh, clean sheets left on each bed. I think of Agatha and how she's gone out of her way to help us and to make us feel welcome. These are a kind people and yet, there is a definite troubling atmosphere attached to this house which I don't understand.

From the terrace below, drifts the sound of Max's guitar, returning me to our conversation in the cafe and the fact I feel closer to him now than I have for a very long while. Even if I couldn't afford it, I'm glad I bought him the guitar. I'm glad it's made him so happy, returning him to the sunny Max of old. I should have known about the bullying at school but chastise myself as I will, I congratulate myself that I've at least I've managed to do some good today. A mystery solved but I can't help thinking… It's only as another, even more baffling, raises its head.

# Chapter Five

"I'm not going…"

"You jolly well are young lady! Agatha asked for you, in particular. You'd hurt her feelings…"

"Who cares!"

"Chloe!" This from Edward, who hates rudeness.

"If she's not going, neither am I…"

"Max…"

"I do so want to go to the party…" Daisy implores.

Father's saying nothing and remembering Agatha's flirtatiousness towards him, I can't blame him. Agatha is proving a handful and, good progress as Father's made from his illness, he's still not fully recovered. He's too old, too set in his ways for romantic involvement. I can't and won't imagine it.

We've become honorary Greeks, sliding into the day so effortlessly, already we feel as if we've been here forever. We're sitting round the breakfast table, me stealing quick, sideways glances towards the irresistible Simon. What must he think of this family he's temporarily landed himself with? He's been quiet since the trip to Lakka. Is he already regretting spending his precious holidays with us, en famille as it were? Last night, after manoeuvring Edward alone, into a corner, I tried to get him to open up about their relationship, entirely unsuccessfully, I admit. Edward can be as tight as a clam when he wants. But I'm increasingly certain that something's wrong.

"We don't have to stay long," I say firmly. "It's kind of Agatha to have asked us…"

From the olive groves below the terrace drifts the sound of a stubborn, irritable roar, a donkey's bray, mixed in with a man shouting angrily. Max jumps up.

"I'll have a look what's up…" he mumbles, obviously relieved to get away.

"I'll come too…" Chloe joins in.

"And me!" Daisy implores, hating to miss out on anything in which her big brother and sister are involved. Shortly, the younger members of our party have disappeared into the shelter of the olive trees, whilst the commotion below only increases in velocity. Edward sighs.

"Should we take a look?"

"They'll be back to tell us what it is, shortly, I expect." I turn eagerly to Simon, it seeming important to me that, on the matter of Milo's party, we should present a united front. "Simon, you must come to the party, too…"

"Oh, I'm sure your Agatha didn't mean to include me in her plans. She doesn't even know me," he answers, doubtfully but smiling at me so warmly, it softens the effect of his refusal.

My stomach executes a double flip. Then I wonder again, if he guesses the effect he has on me. He must be used to women falling at his feet. I wonder what he thinks of women exactly and how he deals with their advances. That particular thought, unpalatable as it is, quells my ardour.

"I'll make fresh coffee," Father says, heaving himself to his feet. Collecting a pile of plates together, Edward hastens after him, unexpectedly leaving Simon and me alone.

"Simon, I know it's none of my business, why, I scarcely know you but… Are you sure you and Edward are quite alright?" I burst out.

Tactless, impulsive, ill-thought out. Motor-mouth, that's me and I'm surprised he answers me.

"Of course, we're alright," he answers huffily.

"I still worry about him. Edward, I mean. We were together for such a long time. I should hate it if he were to get hurt!" I career on; only deepening the hole I've dug myself. Am I warning him off? Or trying to make myself feel better? But I mean what I say. He hurts Edward at his peril and he needs to know this. I glance up quickly and see his gaze narrowing, speculatively.

"The break-up of your marriage must have been a difficult time for you both. Had you no idea…I mean that…well…?"

"That he was gay?"

"Yes, exactly."

I have no need to confide in this man but I'm sure Edward will have told him pretty much everything already. In any case, there's no point trying to evade the issue. I struggle for words to explain exactly what my marriage was like. I knew something was wrong. I'd sensed it for a long time but because I didn't know what to do, I chose to ignore it. Ostrich and sand spring to mind.

"I was shocked. Everyone was shocked and yet we shouldn't have been, not really because then, things that hadn't made sense, made perfect sense."

"It's great you've remained such good friends…"

"There are the children to think about. Edward's their father. He loves them. It's so much easier this way, for all our sakes…" My voice trails to a halt. I've wandered away from the conversation I'd intended, in other words, Simon's intentions towards Edward. But how old fashioned that sounds! My every intuition tells me that, just like Edward, Simon doesn't like talking about himself, indeed, will do anything to evade it. I have my work cut out but before I can even try to discover more, Max reappears, hurrying back towards the terrace, his face filled with excitement.

"You'd better come quickly," he shouts before he reaches us. "Boadicea's in Tomas's vegetable patch…"

"Oh Heaven's…"

I knew that donkey would be trouble. Max hurries back and Simon and I spring up and hurry after him, through the cool depths of the trees and down towards the vegetable plot or what was once a vegetable plot. I can't believe what's happened to it in the interim.

I cannon to a halt and my hand rises to my mouth, stifling a cry of dismay as I take stock of the unbelievable destruction one relatively determined donkey can create. Plants smashed and trampled, canes broken in half and strewn the length and breadth of the garden, the whole plot looking as if it's a grazing ground for elephants. A low stone wall at the top of the rows has tumbled over, onto a row of peas, damaging them beyond salvation, whilst the tomato plants, next row on, lie broken on the ground.

And in the middle of such carnage, hat tipped rakishly to one side, a strand of tell-tale carrot dangling from her lips, Boadicea stands benignly munching, mistress of all she surveys, the length of frayed rope around her neck bearing witness to her crime. At sight of us, her friends, her lips draw back from her large, tombstone teeth and she brays a happy welcome. In a vain effort to get her to budge, Tomas, standing behind her, is pummelling her fat rump with his balled fist, all to no avail. And then, just when we think there's no moving her, contrary as ever, she decides she's had enough and sets off at a trot. Hooting with delight, Max and Chloe, a gleeful Daisy in tow, set off in hot pursuit, disappearing quickly into the depths of the trees at the top end of the garden. Silence descends.

"Tomas, I'm sorry," I murmur, inadequately, not even sure if he understands. Perhaps my voice touches a chord for he sighs heavily, meanwhile regarding me with heavy, doom-laden eyes. There's nothing he can say, nothing anyone can say. Months of hard labour set to nought.

Simon, with no more idea than I what to do, runs an exasperated hand through his hair.

"Look… Why don't you give Max and Chloe a hand in catching the damn thing," he says, turning to me, "whilst I help this chap here… Tomas, isn't it… to get things straight…as much as we can."

That's the problem, there'll be no repairing this damage. But as a plan there's no faulting it and unable to come up with another, in any way its equal, that's what we decide to do. It's good of Simon to trouble himself when he's on holiday…as am I, I concede, ruefully, yet hardly giving that a thought either. Common decency directs that we should help.

I leave Tomas and Simon to make a start on clearing the garden, and hurry away, after my offspring, guided by gusts of insensitive laughter, drifting through the trees towards me. Emerging into the open, I hurry through a clearing and across a criss-cross pathway, finally catching up with them in a flower-strewn, slanting meadow, dotted with olive trees, giving sudden, abrupt and tantalizing glimpses of the sea below, shimmering like sparkling glass. I could forgive anyone anything for these glimpses of heaven, even Boadicea for trashing Tomas' garden, his pride and joy. They take my breath away but then, I'm learning that so much of Paxos has exactly this effect.

Boadicea has come to a halt and stands, chewing placidly on a large, saucer-like, ocean-blue flower she's torn from a plant climbing the low stone wall, the outer boundary of Cassiopeia, I realise. She's dug her hooves in again for despite all Chloe's coaxing and gentle encouragement, Daisy's stroking of her muzzle and soft crooning – donkey language she assures me - and Max tugging manfully on the frayed rope around her neck, she refuses to budge, merely watching their efforts with interest but with obviously no intention of losing her hard-fought battle for freedom.

Finally, Max loses patience and throws down her reins in disgust. He leans back, hands thrust in his pockets, against what I see now is a sort of corrugated iron shack, built by the apex of the wall. I wonder what it is and to whom it belongs. To whoever owns this property, I muse, a man or a woman whose identity, I have no need to remind myself, I'm no nearer discovering.

Aware of my quick frown of interest, Max turns and regards the shed curiously before taking the trouble to search around it for a way in. It's here, it must have a purpose. He drags at the rough door he discovers at the side, which promptly falls off with a clatter, allowing him the luxury of peering into the gloomy interior. His interest however, is short-lived for disappointingly, all that's revealed, lurking in the dark like some long forgotten prehistoric monster, is what we perceive to be an incredibly rusty motor-cycle, unworthy of the protection the shed provides.

"What a pile of old rubbish," Max states baldly.

I can't disagree and it must have been here for donkeys' years, literally, its presence neither here nor there and certainly nothing to do with us. Max props the door back up again and I return my attention to the problem presently presenting itself, namely Boadicea and what exactly we're meant to do with her.

Impasse has been reached but then, just when I'm thinking of sending Chloe to fetch Agatha, like manna from heaven, we hear an irate shout and turn to see that lady herself, hastening towards us at a stumbling trot, ill-suited to her frame - which only a kind person would describe as bonny. Others might say plump but not to her face, I conjecture.

That she's hot and bothered and out of breath is plain to see and no wonder. Boadicea shuffles her hooves and I swear that donkey's laughing. Agatha slaps her smartly on the rump.

"Go home!" she roars, then stands, hands on ample hips, watching as, miraculously, Boadicea trots straight off, heading towards a five-barred gate located at the top end of the field and leading onto the path heading villagewards. Her owner exhales a long, deep breath of exasperation.

"She's made a terrible mess of Tomas' field," I hazard.

"I make it right…"

"I hope you can, Agatha…"

"Tomas good man and understand…"

"It's a dreadful thing to have happened on the day of Milo's party."

"You come to Milo's party, too?" she enquires.

"We'll be delighted," I answer, if hardly daring to look at Chloe and Max. Agatha appears to pick up on my reticence and the exact cause of it, for her gaze slides towards Max, her frown of disapproval taking in the shed behind him.

"I forget…Is still here…" she says.

"There's only a pile of old rust inside."

"Is old bike…army vehicle…from war…"

"A Greek army bike…?" Max enquires and all ears at this. As a little boy, he was obsessed with planes, tanks, engines, anything to do with the wartime armed forces, recollecting me instantly to rainy afternoons and Air Fix models, lovingly constructed. We hadn't realised what we'd found.

"Is Italian…a Benelli…from time of Italian occupation of Ionian Isles. Bad time. Bad people…"

"But what's it doing here? I never realised Paxos was occupied during the war…." I chime in and my interest aroused.

Agatha frowns. "Before Italians switch sides and German Army took over. Long, long ago and bad time for our history. Much sorrow and hardship amongst our people…" She breaks off and I think there's more she could tell me, if only she wanted to. I'm ashamed I know so little about the war but given the bike's an unhappy reminder of a time that people would surely rather forget, I wonder what it's still doing here.

Before I have chance to pump her further, however, almost as if she fears that I might, she utters a hasty goodbye and with voluble exhortations she'll see us later, she hurries after Boadicea. Reaching the gate, she lets them both out, allowing us to follow her further progress via her head, bobbing along the other side of the wall. And then she's gone, Boadicea with her and there's no reason for any of us to remain here.

Back at Tomas' vegetable plot, I'm relieved to see that progress has been made and that Edward and Father have now joined the working party. Tomas is raking the broken plants into a heap and Edward and Simon are digging the ground over. Father meanwhile, hat plonked firmly on his head, sits atop an upturned pail, issuing instructions. With deep content, he's dragging on one of his favourite cheroots which dangles between his lips. He's incorrigible. This, when he knows my opinion about smoking and, even worse, exactly what the doctors have told him. He will live his life exactly how he wants and no-one is going to argue him out of it, not even me, his only child. He smiles easily. Charm goes a long way but not always quite far enough.

"Bryony, my love… There you are…"

"Yes, here I am…"

Having established that fact to everyone's satisfaction and throwing him a look indicating my deep displeasure, I join in with the clearing up, pleased to see Max and Chloe follow suit, so that shortly, with all these extra hands, in as little time as possible, Tomas' garden is restored to some kind of order. Tomas is voluble in what I presume to be his thanks but as he speaks in his native tongue, it's impossible to interpret. However, we get the gist and I'm pleased we've made a connection with him, an old man who seems as timeless as the sea.

He departs back to the village and our party returns to our villa. It'll soon be time for Milo's party and having established the fact that this family, Simon now included, are all to attend it, I descend to the kitchen to make a start on lunch.

Greek music is playing, foot-tapping music, dominated by the inevitable guitar-like bouzouki and the party is already in full swing. It's late afternoon, Agatha has shut up shop and in her tiny living-room, tables and chairs are pushed back against the wall and the French windows are flung open, allowing access into a heavenly flowered garden beyond.

Greeks certainly know how to party and the food and drink are flowing. I had no idea the village was so populated, for given the numbers present, I assume everyone in it must be here, so many people crammed into so tiny a space, it's impossible to move. I can't help noticing an initial drawing away from us amongst the party-goers, a tangible feeling of reserve concerning our presence here but thankfully it's gone just as quickly as it's arisen. Perhaps I've imagined it. I've no idea what we're doing here, English people in a foreign land but then Agatha sees us and pushes her way through the crush towards us, her smile enveloping all our little party which, after much bullying on my part, numbers even Father, despite all his grumblings that Agatha intends to make mincemeat of him. He's probably right.

"You have come," Agatha beams, her gaze alighting on Father and worryingly sticking there.

"Unfortunately," he mumbles, under his breath.

"It's kind of you to have asked us, Agatha," I gush, throwing him a warning look, a reminder he's promised to be on his best behaviour. Proudly, Agatha takes us and introduces us to a frail figure, sitting hunched in an upright chair, by the windows, an Orthodox priest, tenderly clasping an alarmingly large glass of wine, from which, now and then, he takes an appreciative swig and smacks his lips. Just like the pictures of priests I've seen in travel brochures, he has a chimney pot hat and black over-cassock and a wild, straggly, grey beard.

Agatha takes his hand and kisses it profusely.

"Father Ignatius, these people are English and staying at Cassiopeia…"

The information brings a quizzical look winging to the ancient face. He's as old as

Methuselah and I suddenly wonder, awkward as it would be on such brief acquaintance, if he would be the one to talk to about our villa.

"I am pleased to meet you, my children," he intones softly, in impeccable English, his kindly gaze including all our party, even Chloe, in full Goth regalia. A wise old man who has seen much of life, I suspect.

"We're pleased to meet you, too, Father," Simon responds, politely.

"Perhaps I'll see you in church on Sunday," Father Ignatius replies, innocently enough but then he chuckles quietly to himself. When he laughs, his whole-body shakes.

"Quite possibly, Father," Edward replies boldly and who, back home, often goes to church.

Not much of a church goer myself, I can only mumble a hasty 'perhaps, Father,' softening my words with a smile. Shortly, we all have a drink in our hand and we begin to mingle.

I'm delighted to see Max sticks with Edward, the pair ending up squashed together in a corner, deep in conversation. Shamelessly, Daisy stands listening in, her gaze swinging avidly from one face to the other. Max's guitar is propped up beside him, indeed, has hardly left his side since we discovered it, bringing a change in my son's demeanour nothing short of miraculous.

Simon, meanwhile, has disappeared with Father, into the throng outside, giving me ample opportunity to tab-hang on a developing conversation between Chloe and the birthday boy, Milo, who has finally managed to disengage himself from a group of young people, his friends I presume, to make his way towards her. Her outfit today is bondage pants and a tastefully ripped tee-shirt, below a spiked collar, the whole off-set by her terrible hair and black lip-stick and nail polish. The Lord knows what people must think of her and of us, by association but the fact she's agreed to come surely says something in her favour. I can tell she's enjoying Milo's reaction. Recollecting now their first and only meeting so far, it occurs to me she's dressed as she is on purpose, especially to shock him. She's certainly managed that. I sidle nearer.

"Have I got cabbage stuck on my teeth?" she demands, rudely.

Milo frowns. "You eat before you get here?" he asks, ignoring her snort of derision. His gaze roams over her face as gently, he brushes her lips with a tentative finger. "Is beautiful. Why?"

"Why, what?"

"Why you hide your face?"

"I'm a Goth, dumbo," she answers, scathingly.

"What is this, Goth and dumbo…?"

"It's… Oh, never mind…"

"Is beautiful, your face…" he croons, relentlessly but all the while, looking down at her so tenderly, I could shake her for not responding. She has no answer to his gentle love-makings and for a moment I'm minded to leave her to it but then he laughs softly, a little wickedly and I'm just starting to think I ought to step in, when I become aware of a broad-shouldered figure making his way towards me. Instantly, I forget all about Chloe. It's Simon.

"Penny for them?" he asks, teasingly.

"Hah! They're worth far more than that! Where's Father?"

"Left in Agatha's capable hands…" he returns alarmingly, then, as if the news he's just imparted is of no consequence, his gaze focuses on Edward and he frowns.

"Edward has a few problems to sort out with Max," I say, feeling the need to explain.

"I guess that's what this holiday is about, to iron things out with his children…"

"He so wanted them to meet you…"

"Our relationship is getting rather serious, isn't it," he points out, a reasonable enough observation but one that obviously pains him. If I hadn't guessed it already, I'd know for sure there's something wrong. It's none of my business but I've never let that stop me.

"And you're not ready for the commitment yet," I hazard, meaning it as a question but as soon as the words leave my mouth, seeing it as the statement of fact it undeniably is. He looks so troubled by what I've just said, I have to remind myself it's Edward's corner I'm fighting here.

"That obvious, is it?"

"Perhaps you two need to talk…"

"You'd think so, wouldn't you? Unfortunately, it seems Edward doesn't want to hear what I have to say. I'm afraid he's avoiding me."

"I see," I say, if conceding this puts a whole new slant on the situation, as so far explained to me by Edward. Giving me a chance to digest this unexpected confidence, Simon takes our empty glasses and goes to refresh them at the bar, set up on a table in the corner of the room, fighting his way back through the crowd with admirable tenacity and without spilling a drop.

I take a good swig from my glass. "I think life's very complicated sometimes, Simon."

"Tell me about it," he agrees heavily.

"It would be so much easier if only people would fall in love where they've best chance of receiving it back – but it never quite works out that way, does it?"

"Are you trying to say you know something I don't?" he demands suspiciously.

"Of course not! I know that Edward happens to think an awful lot of you," I venture, cautiously, wondering, meanwhile, given that Edward has spoken to me about this subject in total confidence, how much of it, I ought to divulge.

Throwing caution to the wind, I determine to put my own feelings to one side and to do my very best for Edward. "He thinks you're still hung up on your last relationship and you're not ready yet to make a commitment. I'm guessing this man must have meant a lot to you?" I murmur, charging in like the proverbial bull in the china-shop. I should have known better for I don't even need to register the shocked expression on Simon's face, to tell me I've gone too far. "I'm sorry, it really is none of my business," I stumble, haltingly and back-tracking as fast as I can.

Simon leans forward. "Rather ironic, isn't it? Wanting to make a commitment to someone who has no intention of settling down, only they never bother to tell you so, whilst Edward here, hardly gives a bloke time to recover from one disastrous affair before determining to plunge him headlong into another. You're too right, life is complicated."

There's a bitterness in his voice that makes me treat him to a closer look. He's been hurt, so much is obvious and I don't want him lashing out and hurting Edward because of it. He takes a long swig from his glass and I open my mouth to offer at least some kind of reassurance when suddenly, from the direction of the garden, Father re-appears, Agatha hot on his heels. He's red in the face and his bow-tie is askew, so immediately and naturally, I worry about how much he's had to drink. Plenty by the looks of it and in such a short space of time, it's unbelievable. And then I remember our long and protracted lunch and wonder how much he had before he got here. Father likes a glass of wine with lunch. He likes a glass of wine with everything, particularly when he's on holiday. Seeing me, he beams and pushes through the crowd towards me.

At that moment, the music stops and to fill the gap, Max picks up his guitar and begins to play, laying his gift humbly at our feet as if no one will even notice. Instantly, the babble of voices, the sound of a party in full swing, dies to an appreciative hush and people stop to listen. Soulful, swirling music, so full of emotion, it fills me with pride.

Chloe isn't the only one who's made a conquest. By his side, I see, slightly surprised by it, is the girl from the café, in Gaius, swaying her slim hips in time to the music. Father is swaying too, only nothing to do with the music, merely obeying the instincts of the wine, swilling around his system, reducing the fact of standing upright to a procedure requiring his fullest attention. I seize hold of his arm, waiting impatiently, meanwhile, for Agatha to join us.

"You okay?" she demands.

I smile, guiltily. "Agatha, I'm so sorry and thank you so much for inviting us to this wonderful party but as you can see… Father is a little unwell and I really ought to take him home."

Unwell just about describes it. Agatha's face falls.

"But we have such good time. You not go yet…?"

I'm sorry to disappoint her but I have no other choice. "If you could just mention to Edward, if he wouldn't mind keeping an eye on Daisy…?"

He'll do that instinctively but it puts my mind at rest to remind him. Finally understanding my predicament and that I have no remedy other than to take Father home, Agatha sadly agrees. I'm eternally grateful to Simon who takes hold of his other arm.

"I'll come with you," he says firmly.

"Please…you stay and talk to Edward…don't let this spoil the party…"

"Edward can wait," he replies. Father sways forward.

"Alas! The house of women! It is known to be a lovely and a fearful thing!" he announces to the room in general and to anyone else interested in listening.

There's nothing we can say to it, any of it. Swearing like a trooper under my breath, somehow Simon and I, between us, manage to manhandle him outside and into the fresh air, where he sobers up enough to walk upright between us, in a fairly straight line, along the path between the olive groves. In the bay below, as if in delight at our plight, the sea chuckles whimsically, a musical accompaniment to our laboured progress. Dusk is already falling, hiding our shame.

"There is a pleasure in the pathless woods, there is a rapture on the lonely shore…"

"Is there, indeed!"

"There is society where none intrudes, by the deep sea and the music or its roar…"

There's really nothing I can say to that either and I am only too relieved when Cassiopeia rears into view. Home and thank goodness. Inside, we get him upstairs to bed, leaving him fully clothed, if minus shoes and hat, fast asleep and snoring, blissfully unaware of our embarrassment. There's nothing else to do, only let him sleep it off, leaving me to tackle his behaviour in the morning.

"His drinking is becoming a problem," I say, miserably, to Simon, once we're back downstairs again. Just in case he hasn't noticed it already which would be the biggest surprise of the lot. I find a bottle of wine and scarcely registering the irony, I pour us each a badly needed glass.

"Perhaps he's just unhappy," he points out, taking a meditative swallow. "Edward's mentioned about his heart attack. It must be difficult, intimations of mortality and all that."

"I'm wondering now, if he's always drunk too much and it's just that I never noticed."

"We can't be responsible for another's actions, even those of our parents," he points out gently, and leaving me thinking, how easy he is to talk too and how I understand now, exactly why Edward's fallen in love with him. We've wandered out onto the terrace, into the rapidly falling darkness and I'm starting to worry about Daisy – and Chloe too, come to that, left with Milo, apparently, hell bent on seduction.

"Edward will remember about Daisy, won't he?" I moan, beginning to fret.

It's a stupid question. "Of course, he will," Simon soothes me, "but…I don't suppose anyone thought to take a torch for the walk back? It's dropping dark. If it would set your mind at rest, I'll fetch the one from the kitchen and take a stroll back that way…"

"No, I'll go…that is…if you wouldn't just mind keeping an eye on Father…"

Simultaneously, we both put our drinks down on the table and turn to fetch the torch. Clumsily, in the process, we knock into each other and all at once, and entirely unexpectedly, the air is charged with an unmistakeable electricity. Instinctively, Simon puts his arms out to steady me and accidentally, I'm sure it's accidentally, I stumble into them. Of course, it's accidentally and nothing at all to do with the fact we've both had too much to drink. Simon has no interest in girls, for heaven's sake, I hastily remind myself but then, his arms close around me and suddenly, my heart is beating a rapid tattoo against my chest.

He's gazing down at me and worse, with the sort of expression that in anyone else, I might read the world. His head inclines and wonderfully, our lips meet and linger.

Edward, please forgive me but it feels so right is all I can think. It feels so right.

"Well what have we here…" a low voice drawls, behind us.

I'd know that voice anywhere and I can't believe I'm hearing it now. Like scalded cats, Simon and I spring apart and I swing around to find myself face to face with Jake.

# Chapter Six

Not waiting for an introduction, Simon hurries away down the steps to the kitchen, to fetch the torch, which is kept hung up at the back of the kitchen door. Jake smirks. Re-emerging moments later, Simon bolts past him to the lower terrace and the path beyond, leaving us alone. The silence grows painfully, until, that is, I decide attack is the best form of defence.

"What the hell are you doing here?" I snap, hardly in a frame of mind to listen to his answer.

There's no adequate answer because nothing is currently making much sense. My emotions are in turmoil. Shocked from my embrace with Simon - and what an embrace, from a man who professes to have no interest in girls! He couldn't possibly… I mean, why would he and what on earth is Edward going to say if he ever finds out? That thought makes me cold all over. Edward who loves Simon more than anyone he's ever loved in his life. How could I and how could Simon? I decide, there and then, that Edward must never find out.

Jake drops his holdall to the floor. "I could ask the same of you," he says, deliberately, nodding his head in Simon's direction. "Who's lover-boy?"

"Simon's not my lover!"

"Sure didn't look it from where I was standing…"

I have no recourse but to stand on my dignity and nip this thing in the bud.

"Simon's nothing to do with me. And in any case, what you saw, or thought you saw, is none of your business," I answer frostily. "It was a mistake, something that was never meant to happen. We've both had too much to drink."

"Ah, the evils of alcohol…"

"Don't you take that high-handed tone with me!"

Jake says nothing to this, only looks, knowingly, reminding me exactly why, by the time our relationship had crashed to its natural conclusion, we couldn't even bear to be in the same room.

"You've still not told me what you're doing here…"

"I'm following your example and taking a little impromptu holiday. What's good for the goose and all that. A little sunshine, relaxation and fresh sea air, what's not to like…"

"And Burleigh Rovers?"

"What about Burleigh Rovers?"

"Isn't it pre-season training? Given what I've been reading in the papers, you're in enough trouble as it is…"

"My, you have been busy…"

"I could hardly miss the coverage it's been given. Jake, how could you? Whatever's Daisy going to think…?"

"Keep Daisy out of this…"

"The longer you keep away, the worse it'll be. They've already fined you thousands…"

"No sweat! So what? It's only money. There's plenty more where that came from…"

We face each other like two stags at bay and inconsequentially, it crosses my mind, what it must be like to have so much money, a fine constituting more than most people could earn in a year, fails to make the slightest impression, or deter this man from doing exactly as he pleases. Jake always does as he pleases and bad luck to anyone who happens to get in his way. Experience has taught me so much. But I digress, failing to pin him to the sticking point, as it were, always a dangerous precedent where Jake's concerned.

"Where are you staying?" I demand, wondering why he looks so put out at what, after all, is an innocuous enough question.

"You didn't get my card?"

"What card?"

"The one I sent, asking if you could put me up for a day or two…"

In view of Daisy and in case of any emergencies, fool that I am, I told him we were going away and gave him our address, here in Paxos, never imagining for one moment he'd put himself on a plane and come here. "I've never received a card. There is no card…"

"Well, I'm here now, anyway…"

"You can't stay!"

"Come on, love, this place is big enough to house a whole football team, reserves to boot. All I want is somewhere to lay my head for a night or so…"

"There's a perfectly good hotel in Gaius…"

We're interrupted by a child's excited scream as Daisy hurtles across the terrace and throws herself into her father's arms. She's followed by Edward and Simon.

"Daisy, girl…" Jake crows, equally as delighted. He swings her up and round and hugs her tightly to him before setting her back on her feet, reminding me sadly, of the natural affection that exists between them and which normally, I do my best to encourage. Jake isn't Daisy's fault.

"Daddy! Daddy! I didn't know you were here!"

"I'm just fixing up with Mummy where I'm staying…"

"But you'll stay here! Mummy! Please, please let Daddy stay…"

Over the top of my daughter's head, my gaze meets Jake's. It's unforgiveable he's using a child to get his own way but he's manoeuvred me into a corner and if I don't do what he wants, Daisy will be upset.

"We were already on our way back. Max and Chloe are staying on at the party…" Edward murmurs, pleasantly. His gaze wanders uneasily towards Jake. "Jake… This is a surprise," he observes, if in a tone of voice implying it isn't a pleasant one.

"Edward… There you are," Jake returns, his gaze flicking towards Simon. "Aren't you going to introduce us?"

Thankfully, Edward, as usual, takes it all in his stride. "Of course, you two haven't met yet. This is Simon, my partner. Simon, this is Jake, Daisy's father…"

Hardly surprisingly, there's an awkward pause, as if no one knows quite what to say next. Simon looks as if he's wishing himself any place else and Jake shoots me a glance full of a malevolent, if slightly perplexed, enjoyment. Simon and I need to talk and sooner rather than later but this is hardly the time or the place. It's amazing how quickly we've both sobered up. Shock, I expect. Sensing an atmosphere, he can't understand, only that Jake is somehow involved and Jake always causes trouble, Edward frowns.

"Mummy, pleeeaaassseeee can Daddy stay?" Daisy bursts out.

There's little else I can do but agree. Hoping I convey at least a little of my displeasure, I glare at Jake. "But only for a couple of nights. Daddy has other plans after that, haven't you, Jake…?"

I'm relieved to crawl into bed. It's been some day and I'm still reeling from the atmosphere on the terrace before we turned in, caused by Jake witnessing my crazy moment of passion with Simon. What fun he's had at our expense, even if his malice, for some reason or other, has been mostly directed at Edward. 'Edward and Simon look so good together. He's so pleased Edward has found someone…didn't we all think, it's about time Edward settled down?' And all spoken in the tone of voice, hinting at some hidden agenda of which only he knows, and which he drew me into by a series of knowing looks.

I could kill him and if it wasn't for the fact that he's Daisy's father, and that she's desperate for him to stay, I'd order him to leave Cassiopeia right now. I've put him up in the smallest back bedroom, situated on the top floor, more a cubby hole really and I only wish I could have put him outside, in a shed or somewhere similar – far away from the rest of us. He's always known how to get under my skin and I can't believe, even given that at the time, I was still reeling from the catastrophic ending to my marriage, I was ever gullible enough to fall for him. He can be charming and, oddly enough, he has a vulnerable side he doesn't show to many. It was this, I think, that drew me to him and made me put up with the rest, far longer than I ought. The affairs and reckless behaviour, the not knowing where he was and what he was up to, at any given time of night or day.

Given his reckless disregard for other people's feelings, I guess deep down, Jake must be unhappy. Perhaps, because I was hurting over my marriage, I recognised his pain and thought I could do something to help him. I'm not exactly sure and I'm no psychologist. Sometimes, our behaviour fails to stand up to scrutiny and I'm afraid my affair with Jake is another of the madnesses to which, as I grow older, I'm becoming increasingly prone. It's too late now to wish I'd never met him and I can only console myself with the one happy outcome of our brief liaison, which is Daisy, living proof that good can emerge from bad.

Unfortunately, uncomfortably as all this sits in my mind, Jake isn't even my main problem because even worse than this, is how I've allowed my feelings to get tangled up with Simon. Simon, who is gay and Edward's lover. What does that say about a man prepared to toy with the affections of the woman Edward was once married too and has children by? What does it say about me?

I can't bear to examine my own behaviour. It's alright assuring myself it was only a momentary weakness but deep down, I know it's more than that.

I'm lonely, desperate even, an accident waiting to happen. I love Edward like a brother and I wouldn't hurt him for the world.

It's the early hours before I hear Chloe and Max letting themselves into the house, giggling together like the young school children they once were, before stumbling off to their respective beds. It sets me wondering about Milo and the girl from the water-front café and if both my nearly grown-up children are about to embark on their first love affairs. There's nothing I can do about this, either, other than accept the fact they're growing up and that I'm growing older and that's the way it always has been and will be for ever more.

The villa sinks back into its comforting silence, broken only by the sound of the cicadas in the garden below, drifting in through my open window. A bat squeaks. An owl hoots. The night is hot and airless and it's not helping my efforts to sleep. I try counting sheep. I try mindfulness. I try attempting to kid myself all's well in my crazy world, the most ridiculous logic of all.

Finally, and reluctantly I give up, rise from my tangled sheets, throw on my dressing-gown and steal downstairs. Tea. Sometimes, tea is the only answer and in any case, after all that wine, my mouth feels like the bottom of the proverbial parrot's cage. Who was it, who first knew what the bottom of a parrot's cage felt like, that's what I'd like to know. I boil the kettle, make tea with a tea-bag and sit at the kitchen table to drink it, my hands curled comfortingly around the mug. This holiday isn't turning out as I'd expected and that's upsetting, particularly as I came away to solve my problems but all I've managed to achieve so far, is to create a whole lot more.

Wasn't life ever thus!

Startling me from my reverie, I hear a noise and I'm just beginning to wonder what ghosts my night-time wanderings have disturbed when, to my relief, Father appears, stumbling into the kitchen, fully dressed and just awoken from his drunken slumber. It only reminds me of yet another problem, the fact that he's drinking too much. Pot and kettle but what the heck. We all need our support mechanisms but the trick is, not to let them get out of hand. At least now, thankfully, he looks relatively sober.

"Tea?" I ask.

"Please." He sits, resting his head on his hand, trying to pretend he hasn't the mother of all hangovers.

It serves him right.

"Father, this has got to stop."

"What, my love?"

"You know perfectly well what. Are you alright?" I ask, more gently, a stupid question when I know that he's not and that if he doesn't deviate from the path on which he's currently set upon, sooner rather than later, he will never be alright again.

"Always laugh when you can. It is cheap medicine," he observes, taking a contemplative sip of his tea.

"Do not quote Byron at me…"

"Darling girl…"

"Or try to get around me," I tell him, sternly. "You're drinking too much and when you've only just recovered from a serious illness. You know what the doctors said…"

"Hah! And I'm to accept doctors know everything?"

They know very little in my experience but that's not the point. As usual, we're going around in circles, a natural occurrence when Father determines on avoiding an unpalatable subject.

The night settles like a mantle around us, sign of the island gathering itself before rousing its inhabitants to its worldly concerns. Perhaps it invites unexpected confidences, breaking through the barrier a parent more normally raises before a child. Question and answer, discipline and obedience, each of us trying to buck the trend. Like Chloe and Max, I think.

He sits across from me, this old man with whom I've shared a lifetime, when I become aware of the oddest of feelings that we're no longer father and child, related by ties of blood and history but rather, two supposedly grown-up people who've both had difficulties of late, none of their fault or making. Father's illness. Me and Mikey. Me and the children. Me and life. We're struggling for survival and truly, this holiday has arrived only just in time. We're sitting together like this because we want to and because, even if we'd rather die than admit it, amongst the arguments and the frictions, the sheer cussedness on his side and yes, the inherited stubbornness on mine, we enjoy each other's company. We're English and thus full of repression, the bane of our race and it occurs to me, we would do well to take the Greek example and occasionally let our feelings out.

"Why? Why are you drinking so much?"

"Youth goes by in a blink," he murmurs, rather surprisingly, a fact we all know but probably don't consider enough. "And then there's nothing left, only to grow old disgracefully. A drink helps soothe the pain, keeps the abyss at bay…"

"Or brings it nearer, you do realise?" I retort and seeing now with a remarkable and painful clarity how much I love this old man and how much I have to be grateful to him for. Difficult as it is, I have to give my thoughts fresh air.

"Dad, I…I…know how you've always tried to do your best for me and how difficult it must have been at times. I mean whilst I was growing up and with Mother running off to join the hippies. Never mind having the business to build up and all that responsibility. I really don't know how you managed it…"

He laughs, more a snort than a chuckle. "Neither did I at times…"

"You deserve this time in your life and the chance to enjoy it. You have so much to look forward to…"

"I can take it…or leave it, you know, the booze…"

"Then leave it a bit…or at least cut down."

We're not a family given to overly familiar demonstrations of affection. He grins amiably and briefly squeezes my hand, lying flat on the table, an action so transitory, I half think I've imagined it.

"For you, dear girl, anything," he says.

Can I believe him? Probably not but, for the moment, it has to be enough. I've broached the subject and laid down some ground rules and hopefully some of it will have stuck. Even this little progress must have settled me, for after we've finished our tea, we return to our respective beds, where I drop off at once, into a deep and refreshing sleep, the type of sleep, moreover, the product of a conscience at ease with itself – an ideal at which I aim and usually fail miserably. Perhaps I've managed to convince myself, none of last night was any of my fault or making. I didn't kiss Simon, Simon kissed me and in that, lies the world of difference…

I don't wake until broad daylight is pouring through the window, slapping my face with an urgent hand. I've overslept but thinking of Jake, of Simon and of Edward, I'm not all that keen to face the day. Reality strikes and I leap out of bed, pausing only to don the uniform shorts and tee-shirt before rushing downstairs. Out on the terrace, breakfast is eaten, pots are in the process of being cleared and Max and Chloe are beating a hasty retreat.

"Morning, Ma…"

"Can't stop, just on our way out…"

"But…"

"Milo and Alex… We're spending the day on Alex's father's boat…"

Alex must be the girl in the café but they don't stop long enough to confirm or deny it. I barely have chance to register the fact my children can manage to function on so little sleep, or even more amazingly that as he passes me, Max plonks a loving kiss on my cheek, before they head off towards the lower terrace and disappear out of sight. Thankfully, there's no sign of Jake.

"Where's Daisy?" I demand, of Father, who is pouring himself a coffee.

Edward smiles. "Jake's taken her into Gaius," he chips in, before Father can answer me. "They've left Jake's car and walked. He said to give you a rest…"

"Without my permission? In this heat?" I screech, like any common fishwife. Father winces and throws me a reproachful look. But Jake has no business taking Daisy anywhere without asking me first. "That's far too far for Daisy, for heaven's sake!"

"Nonsense, it'll do her good," Edward soothes. "Jake is her father, love…"

"Biologically speaking," I agree, if thinking to myself, not in any other way of use to the poor child.

Simon disappears with a pile of pots and with such a sheepish air, I'm convinced he's avoiding me. But what can either of us say about the previous evening that can in any way put it right?

"We thought we'd spend the day exploring the island," Edward informs me, happily and pressing blithely on. "Why don't you come with us, Bry? It would do you good to get away…"

A whole day in Simon's company is surely the last thing either of us could want or contemplate.

"No, that's okay…but thanks all the same..." I mumble, hastily, having the grace to blush.

I summon up courage to snatch a word with Simon before he leaves, cornering him in the kitchen, when I go to make my breakfast. "We need to talk," I hiss, for which I receive an odd glance from Edward, who is standing at the kitchen table fastening the haversack. Almost imperceptibly, Simon nods and then he's gone, heading out of the door to the car, leaving a lingering impression he's relieved to get away so relatively unscathed.

Heaving the haversack onto his shoulder, bidding me a hasty goodbye, Edward hurries after him. Father apart, I'm left alone and I'll just have to make the best of it. Father and I make no more mention of our midnight confidences. What needed to be said has been said and we're both content to leave things as they are. Instead, I make a hasty breakfast of fruit and orange juice, only lingering long enough to ensure he's comfortably ensconced in a chair, on the terrace, plumped up with cushions and with book and coffee-pot to hand, before I set off for Gaius. I'm on Jake's war-path. Someone else with whom I need a heart to heart and there's no time like the present.

As I wander between sleepy olive groves, the sea gurgles and splashes beneath my path and is a musical accompaniment to my footsteps, disassociating me from memories of Jake's untimely arrival and allowing me, instead, to examine, in the warm light of day, over exactly which precipice Simon and I were about to hurl ourselves last night. It was nothing, of course, a momentary aberration, surely understandable, considering we'd both had a fair bit to drink, Simon to the point where it led him beyond his inclinations, to a place he surely never meant to go.

And what am I to make of my own behaviour? I'm obviously missing Mikey, more than I would have believed possible. So much sun, sea air and relaxation, my thoughts were bound to turn to love and for lack of alternative, my affections just so happened to settle on Simon. Simon, who, because of Edward, I know full well, is strictly out of bounds. And then another thought strikes me. Perhaps, deep down, hurt by Mikey's desertion, I don't want another liaison with all its consequent risks of being hurt and thus I settled on Simon as someone to worship from afar, without the worry of entanglement. The fact that not only has he guessed my feelings but shockingly returned them was never on the agenda and has naturally thrown me. So, I deceive myself.

I've reached the port and I dawdle along the waterfront, admiring the boats, moored on the quayside, consoling myself with the fact I can sort things out with Simon later, a simple conversation in which we'll surely agree, last night was a mistake that must never, ever be allowed to happen again.

Eyes alert for sight of Jake and Daisy, I carry on into Gaius, where I soon discover, this busy, sun-bright morning, the town is alive with tourists and day-trippers and trying to find anyone, is a little like looking for the needle in the proverbial haystack. But for once, luck is with me, for no sooner have I reached the market square than I see them, seated under a bright awning outside the café, nearest the waterfront, Daisy's bright yellow tee-shirt and sun-hat, helping me to pick her out. She sees me and waves excitedly, alerting Jake, who turns and smirks across at me, an action engendering in me the usual mixture of dislike and wonder I ever managed to get tangled up with him. For Daisy's sake, I do my best to put my feelings aside and yet, the moment he's within earshot, I'm still unable to help firing off an angry volley.

"You had no business taking Daisy. You didn't even ask. How dare you!" I retort, reaching him and yanking out a chair, which I sink into thankfully. It's hot and I'm in need of sustenance. Ignoring my rudeness, Jake signals the waiter and in perfect Greek, orders me coffee and cake, once again wrong-footing me, an action he's perfected over the years.

"It seemed a shame to disturb you, particularly after you'd been so busy yesterday..."

Is that an edge to his voice? Certainly, there's a malicious enjoyment flitting across his face. Truly, my conscience is troubling me, for other than what he saw on the terrace last night, Jake knows nothing about me and Simon. I squash my temper and take a gulp of coffee.

"I just need to know where Daisy is, at all times of the day, that's all I'm saying..."

"Perfectly safe and sound, as you can see..."

"Daddy's taking us to the beach. Come with us, Mummy. Pleeaassee come with us..."

"I can't, darling, I'm sorry. I need to go back and keep an eye on Grandpa..."

"Nonsense, the old curmudgeon's perfectly capable of looking after himself," Jake intercedes.

He's done it again, neatly trapping me and landing me in a situation I can't get out of without disappointing Daisy. He knows I'll do anything not to disappoint Daisy.

"And how long exactly, will you be staying in Paxos, Jake?" I grind out between gritted teeth.

"Oh, a day or two. You know how it is…"

"You're not going home yet, Daddy?"

"What and pass up chance of spending time with my little princess? Not on your life, I'm not…"

The fact that back home, in England, this man passes up on so many opportunities of spending time with his little princess, hardly needs pointing out and especially not in front of said princess. Perhaps I should be grateful he's spending time with her now. I restrain myself to a knowing look, from which he reads my thoughts exactly. His face flushes up. I take a slug of coffee and steady myself.

"What are you doing here, Jake? You can't expect the club to put up with you missing pre-season training for very much longer. They'll be throwing the book at you one of these fine days…"

"You think I don't know that…?"

"Why, Jake? For Heaven's sake, why?"

"Let's just say, back in dear old Blighty, things have become a little uncomfortable."

We shouldn't be having this conversation with Daisy listening in to every word but somehow, now I've started, I can't seem to stop. "A woman, you mean? What happened? Did her husband find out?"

"Trust you to put that interpretation on it…"

What other interpretation could I put on it? I snort, sarcastically. Obviously stung, Jake picks up his cup and drinks deeply before answering me, picking his words carefully. "And what if I said, that this time, it's different. That this time, it just so happens… I've fallen in love," he murmurs, so unexpectedly, his words shock me. But thoughts of Jake in love are bound to sit uneasily when I know, perfectly well, the only person he's ever truly loved, is himself.

"When she's married?"

"Let's just say, she's otherwise engaged…"

At that precise moment, we both become aware of a man hovering by our table, staring at us as if he knows us and can't quite place us. Camera slung around his neck, notebook in hand, he doesn't even have to open his mouth before I have him nailed as a reporter from one of the daily hacks back home. He seizes the camera and it flashes, blindingly, into our faces.

"Mr. Turnbull, I thought it was you. Any comments for my readers concerning your non-appearance at pre-season training…?" he asks, conversationally and as if he fully expects Jake to answer.

With an angry oath, Jake leaps to his feet and before any of us have chance to say another word, he sets off at a smart pace across the square, shortly breaking into a run from which there's no hope of catching him. He's gone, disappeared into one of the many alleyways leading off from the square. In other words, he's run off and left us alone to face music not of our composition. What a heel! I can guess exactly how the press have found out he's here - a holidaymaker at the airport, or on the plane, a football supporter recognizing a familiar face and only too ready to make a quick profit by ringing one of the sleazier publications. Everyone knows about Jake and the trouble he gets himself into. He lives his life in a goldfish bowl and this is one of its consequences.

"Daddy..." Daisy wails, staring balefully after him.

"Would you care to enlighten our readers, Miss?" the reporter demands. His gaze lingers on Daisy thoughtfully. Daisy favours Jake and there's no mistaking who her father is.

"If any pictures of my child appear in your paper, your editor will be hearing from my solicitor," I state heatedly, before leaping to my feet and hustling Daisy away.

I expect him to come after us, surprised when he merely plonks himself down at the vacated table and starts scribbling in his notebook, rubbish, I expect and shortly to be splashed across all the papers. My impression is confirmed when he takes out his mobile, punching in numbers before speaking heatedly to the person on the other end. What a coupe, the elusive Jake Turnbull, star striker for Burleigh Rovers, cornered in Paxos, the last place anyone would have expected to find him!

"I want my Daddy," Daisy mutters, struggling to keep up.

"Daddy's just remembered he has some urgent business to sort out," I soothe her, unconvincingly. "I tell you what, Darling, let's head for the beach and then he can come and find us when he's done."

Daisy is only a little girl and easy to pacify. Half-truths. Evasions. Something I hate to do to her and yet, because of Jake, I'm left with no alternative. What right has he to come here, spoiling our holiday and worse, involving Daisy in his shenanigans!

The beach in Gaius is man-made, a miniscule stretch of golden-orange sand, a little further along the water-front and across from the tiny island of Agios Nikalaos, which forms a natural breakwater and provides shelter for boats passing through the inlet of the harbour. I plonk myself down on a deckchair, meanwhile keeping a watchful eye on Daisy, paddling her feet in the waves whilst consuming the largest ice-cream Gaius can furnish her with, bought from a vendor, strolling along the water-front and who insisted, in pigeon English and to whoever cared to hear it, that it's 'probably the best ice-cream in the whole wide world'.

In this way, we manage to put Jake's behaviour behind us, even to the point where now and then, my little girl forgets to keep a wary eye on the promenade where sooner rather than later, she hopes to see her daddy's loping stride. It's unlikely, poor pet. Jake will long have forgotten her by now but I can hardly tell her this. She has a heel for a father and as she grows older, she'll discover for herself, that throughout life, we all have our crosses to bear. Jake will be hers, perhaps the biggest of all.

As the day wears on and the blisteringly hot sun hangs high in the sky, burning unwary sunbathers to unflattering lobster-pink, it prompts me to persuade Daisy that perhaps I've made a mistake and her daddy must have decided to return to the villa after all. In any case, I really do need to check on Father. Inwardly cursing that yet again, Jake's managed to let down the one person in the whole wide world, he should instinctively put before anyone else, even and especially himself, I hail a taxi to take us back to Cassiopeia.

# **Chapter Seven**

The only good to come out of today is that I've spent time with Daisy, not always as easy as it sounds given the clutter in our lives, even Daisy's, even on holiday. She leaps out of the taxi, running helter skelter through the gate and along the path, longing to tell her Grandpa about the sea and the ice-cream and her daddy who had urgent business to see to and is he back yet?

My heart breaks for her and when I catch up with Jake, hopefully soon, it'll be to give him a piece of my mind – if he hasn't caught the first plane back to England already. Trying to pin Jake down is a waste of time, as I've learned to my cost. I pay the taxi-driver and follow her, meanwhile considering how best, for her sake, I can maintain any kind of a relationship with her father without wanting to brain him.

Reaching the bottom terrace, I glance up towards Cassiopeia, drawn by a movement at my bedroom window and disturbed to see the figure of a young girl, looking out over the trees towards the sea, though she disappears so quickly, I wonder if I've imagined her. She's there and then she's gone. I must have imagined her, either that, or it's Chloe, back from the day's boat-trip already, the strains of Max's guitar, drifting from the upper terrace rather suggesting it. I'm relieved because for a moment there, I was beginning to think I'd seen a ghost, a spirit of the trouble I'm certain haunts Cassiopeia – and haunts me too, leaving me happy and content on a purely surface level, and yet at the same time, deep down, mixed up and emotional, too, I must have picked up on local superstition, the Evil Eye that's supposedly prevalent in these parts and which I've read so much about in the guide books. 'Matiasma', it's called, a curse motivated by jealousy, which once given, can only be lifted by special prayers from a priest. Father Ignatius' kindly features drift to mind and I wonder if he's ever had to lift a curse. I dread to think what he'd say if I told him all my imaginings about Cassiopeia.

Edward and Simon are back and the sight of them relaxing on the terrace over a bottle of wine jolts me back to reality. Simon! As if I could have forgotten the mess we've got ourselves into. Embarrassing as it is, we have to talk, if only to find out where we go from here.

Max stops playing and eases himself up from the floor where he's been sitting cross-legged. Daisy is hovering close by, and with no sign of her wretched father, she's on the verge of tears. I hate Jake sometimes. In guarded words, I hope the adults can decipher, I recount what's happened.

"He had to rush away on business," I finish, lamely but smiling towards Daisy with every ounce of confidence I can muster and who, thankfully and albeit tremulously, smiles back.

Edward, kindly as ever, leaps up and takes her hand.

"Your dad will be back soon, love. I bet he'll be hungry, too. Let's go and get supper underway, shall we?" he encourages and throwing me a look of commiseration, he directs them towards the kitchen.

Embarrassingly aware of Simon, I ask Max if he and Chloe have had a good day.

"The best," he answers hearteningly and looking so like the Max of old, Simon or not, I can't help blessing the impulse that caused me to bring us out here. "Chloe's gone into Gaius with Milo. Alex has had to go into work…" he goes on, more confusingly.

"But that can't be right…" I begin and immediately thinking of the girl at the window, staring out so yearningly, over the tree-tops to the sea beyond. I try to tell him what I've just seen, or thought I've just seen but it's too late. Slinging his guitar across his back, he lopes away, into the villa.

It's too hot and I'm exhausted and that I've allowed my emotions to run away with me is becoming perfectly clear. Simon waves the bottle of wine in my general direction and then pours me a glass from which I take a grateful swig before sinking down into the chair opposite. He appears tanned and relaxed and the day's excursion has obviously done him good. But unless we're to spend the rest of this holiday, tip-toeing around each other, we simply have to talk, a fact, thankfully, we both recognise. There's so much I want to say to him, I've no idea where to start.

There'll never be a better opportunity.

"Where's Father?" I ask.

"Taken a stroll…to clear his head, I think… Don't worry about him. He's quite alright. On top form, as a matter of fact."

That's good to hear but my mind is spinning like a top. Should I apologise, or are apologies down to Simon?

"Er…Simon…"

"Yes, Bryony?"

"Last night… Whatever were you thinking about?" I snap, unforgivably, instantly and understandably, putting him on the defensive.

"What was I thinking about? What were you thinking about?"

"Me?"

"Yes, you."

His voice is raised and someone will hear us if we're not very careful.

"I'm sorry, that was unfair," I mumble, taking another swig of wine, a shot of badly needed moral courage. "Don't let's fall out, that's the last thing we need. But even you must agree last night was never meant to happen and must never happen again. I wouldn't hurt Edward for the world and I'm sure that's the last thing you'd want, too…"

"I don't want to hurt him…"

"We so easily could, Simon."

"What about Jake?"

"What about him?" I ask, misunderstanding. Jake couldn't care less if I slept with the whole of the Burleigh Rovers football team though I can hardly say as much and certainly not to Simon.

"Will he keep it to himself?"

The penny drops. "You mean, how likely is he to tell Edward what he saw?" I puff out my cheeks and take another slug of wine. Warning bells tell me the alcohol's going straight to my head and I should take care over what is, after all, a conversation in need of sober deliberation. "It just depends," I answer, uncertainly.

"On what…?"

"On how much damage he wishes to inflict. Jake likes upsetting people. It boosts his esteem which isn't always as high as it might first appear."

"That's torn it, then."

"Do you think…perhaps…it might be better if you told Edward first, just in case…" My voice trails away. This last is a stray thought I speak aloud but the probable consequences of which are so horrendous, I can't bear to consider it.

"That's a rotten idea," Simon agrees, to my great relief and at least we're in a like mind over this, the most important issue. Edward must never find out. It's hardly as if Simon and I have slept together but Edward is Edward, the sensitive man we both know and love, a man who could take offence in an empty room. "Perhaps you could have a word with Jake?" he proffers, a suggestion which only tells me he doesn't know Jake.

"That's not a good idea and might conceivably make the situation worse."

"Then we'll just have to wait and see what his next move is…"

In other words, the situation is out of our control. "Simon… Why did you kiss me? I mean, I know why I kissed you. Obviously, you're a very attractive man and any woman would be bound to find you…well…desirable…" Colour heats my cheeks but I'm determined to finish what I've started. "I'm not trying to excuse myself. I must admit, I did…do…find you attractive and it wasn't just the wine though that obviously played a big part. I'm lonely, I think and being out here and relaxing, for once, I allowed my imagination to run away with itself. It isn't even as if you like women!"

I think that about sums it up. Simon fixes me with a stare.

"That's just it though, Bryony. I do like women…"

"What…?"

"My last relationship was with a woman…"

"Oh but you said…"

"I didn't say. You simply assumed."

"Oh. Gosh."

"Edward doesn't know, that's all."

"You mean you haven't told him?"

"I thought it would complicate matters. That it was better if he didn't know. He'd only have fretted."

"But isn't that unfair?"

"Probably. I sensed you liked me but if you must know…I'm attracted to you, too."

It takes me a while to absorb this information, never mind the declaration of Simon's feelings towards me, an added complication which, quite naturally, I'd never imagined. "But you love Edward… Edward thinks you're his forever partner. He wants to settle down."

Simon's brows cloud over. "I'm not exactly sure that's what I want," he answers, solemnly. "What about children and a family life? Edward's got that already, with you. I do love him. But being with him shuts the door on a whole aspect of life I want to experience."

"Women aren't brood mares, Simon!"

"That's not what I mean…"

"Couldn't you adopt?"

"It wouldn't be the same and anyway, can you really see Edward going through all that rigmarole again when he's already got Chloe and Max, Daisy, too, in a way…"

I concede he has a point and that he and Edward have some real problems to sort out. He should have been more up front, I think. Furthermore, that it's a dilemma of Simon's own making and one in which I only played the tiniest of bit parts. And then I think, how amazingly hard we try to absolve ourselves of our bad behaviour. This mess is my fault, too.

"You have to tell Edward exactly how you feel," I point out, reasonably.

This conversation has taken place in little above a whisper and Daisy's sudden reappearance from the direction of the kitchen, bearing a bowl of olives, causes us both to resume a more normal air, meanwhile probably only succeeding in making ourselves look as guilty as hell. Lord knows why, when we haven't exactly done anything yet – it was a kiss, that was all, a simple kiss and I don't know why I'm making such a fuss over it. She's followed by Edward who has a tea-towel slung jauntily over one shoulder. He bats his eye-lids at me.

"I was wondering if you'd like to come to church with me tomorrow, Bryony. It's no good asking Simon, the heathen He won't go anywhere near a church. But it would be good to have some company?"

Has he guessed what we've been up too and saint-like, he's offering me a chance of absolution? I treat him to a hard stare and see that, thank goodness, he remains blithely unaware of me and Simon. Reassured, I give the invitation consideration. Even though I've always felt drawn to the church, totally illogically with my lack of belief, back home churches are reserved for weddings and funerals. But I discover that I want to experience everything this island has to offer and considering how guilty I feel, perhaps I ought to go, if only for the peace and quiet to contemplate my behaviour.

Has my heart to heart with Simon helped, or only complicated matters? It's impossible to tell. I'm uncomfortable knowing what I know about Simon when Edward doesn't know, and the sooner this situation is remedied, then the better it will be.

"I'd like that, thank you. But why don't you and Simon go out for lunch afterwards? Take a trip into Gaius? It would be great for you two guys to have some time alone…" The suggestion is clumsy and obvious but this is Simon's cue, his chance to talk properly to Edward over a few, inhibition-releasing glasses of wine. For some reason, having spent the whole day in Edward's company, Simon has so far chosen to keep his problems to himself.

"Mmm, good idea," he agrees, seizing on my initiative. "What do you reckon, Ed?"

Edward smiles. "Yes, why not. You and Daisy would be welcome to join us, Bryony?"

"Thanks but after today's escapade, I've had quite enough of Gaius for the time being. Besides, church apart, Daisy and I are waiting in for your daddy, aren't we, darling? We have one or two problems need sorting, when we finally catch up with him…" Like what he means by turning up here, press pack in tow. And how dare he toy with Daisy's emotions in this way, spoiling her holiday and mine, too, come to that…

It appears that everything is arranged satisfactorily if only it wasn't for Jake. To Daisy's dismay, he fails to put in an appearance, the vacant place setting at the supper table staring up at us accusingly. "He's probably just been waylaid, darling. He'll be back as soon as can be…"

Easy words and I only wish they were true. But the following morning, when I check Jake's room before coming downstairs, it's only to discover his bed unslept in and that despite the clothes spilling out of his overnight bag, the room has about it the empty air, that lacking its occupant, a room takes on so quickly.

At the door, I catch a whiff of familiar after-shave, horribly recalling me to intimate dinners and lazy morning breakfasts in bed, in other words, a scent assaulting me with memories I've no desire to recall. Once upon a time, Jake and I were close, before I saw through him, of course, and discovered what a low-down he really is. I've no idea where he's got to. Selfishly, I hope he's gone home to England to his club and made a start on sorting out his problems. I think of the woman back home he professes to love and I pity her. Another whim, soon to be headed the way of the rest. Jake does have good points, if just for the moment, I fail to remember one.

The faint clang of a church bell drifts across the air. One by one, family begin to emerge downstairs, into the bright, warm, all-enveloping air of a Paxos Summer Sunday morning and we sit down to breakfast.

"You won't mind keeping an eye on Daisy whilst Bryony and I go to church, will you, Simon?" Edward asks easily and to Father's obvious surprise. Knowing my general lack of curiosity about religion, he looks up at me askance from the paper I bought back yesterday from our trip into Gaius. There's plenty in it about Jake and I make a mental note to make sure Daisy doesn't see it.

"Of course, I don't mind," Simon agrees amiably.

Daisy's head shoots up. "Don't need looking after!" she pouts furiously. "I'm going to the beach with Max and Chloe!"

"Hah! You can forget that young lady. You're not tagging along with us this time…"

"Next time, we'll take you next time," Chloe placates. She smiles happily and I notice for the first time and with a sense of shock, how different she looks this morning. It takes a moment for it to sink in exactly what it is. Hair neatly combed, no make-up, shorts topped by a pretty pastel tee-shirt, admirably showing off her tan.

"Oh, but Chloe, you're not dressed in your Goth gear!" I blurt out, tactlessly.

"So?" she snaps straight back.

"So…er… well…nothing. It's just that you look different, that's all…" I nearly say normal and only just stop myself. "But very nice, lovely, in fact,"

I gush, unforgivably. She looks beautiful but I can't find the words to tell her so. Truly, Milo has worked miracles.

Breakfasting on bread and honey, washed down with deliciously strong, piping-hot, Greek coffee, made by other hands than mine, I smile quietly to myself.

Neither Edward or I want to be late. We hurry around the villa, tidying-up, washing pots and making beds and then we set off, an old, once-married couple, myself mindful of Greek sensitivities and dressed conservatively, in a blouse with long sleeves and a long-flowing floral skirt and sandals. My hair is tied back. After the freedom of the last few days, I feel constrained and too hot by far though I console myself, it won't be for long.

As we walk, I cast sideways glances at Edward and imagine what he'll have to say when he hears Simon's confession and if he'll be able to come up with any way round it. Simon wants children and whilst Edward is proud of his brood, I can't envisage him wanting to start parenthood over again. Whichever way I think about it, there's no getting away from the truth. Simon likes women as well as men and may not be willing to give up one for the sake of the other. What that says about him, I'm not quite sure, only that he appears to want his cake and to eat it, too. I wonder where it will leave Edward. Dear Edward, who, unless pushed into a corner by yours truly, is more normally the most faithful and trustworthy of men...

Talking is at least a start and I wish now that we'd talked, too, getting to know each other properly before we plunged so headlong into matrimony. But then, if we hadn't married, there'd be no Chloe and Max and no matter what the difficulties of single parenthood, I can't imagine a world without them. Nothing is as straightforward as it first appears.

A mangy black cat, skeletal thin, bolts across the track in front of us, disappearing over a pile of broken stones into a wilderness of tangled greenery, mixed in with pale-pink and dusky-red flowers that raise their pretty faces towards us. The scent of jasmine, cascading over the front wall of a pastel-lemon painted villa, drifts across from an olive grove in which even more flowers grow.

"Penny for them?" Edward teases.

"Oh…nothing…that is…I was just thinking… How glad I am to be here!" I burst out. "Problems don't seem problems here, as if it doesn't matter whether they're solved or not. Do you feel it, too?"

He grins endearingly. "I do, funnily enough. Take me and Max. I can't believe now I ever thought we didn't get on..."

"Edward…"

"Yes, my love…"

"Don't you think there's something, well, strange about Cassiopeia?"

"Strange, how?" Edward has a way of looking down his nose when he's surprised and he does this now. I've never realised before how it's always irritated me. I knew I'd never be able to explain it.

Regardless, I plough on.

"It's just that… You only have to mention to folk that we're staying at Cassiopeia and you get a reaction – it happened with Agatha and with an old man called Spiro we stopped to speak to on the way into the village. He was fine until we mentioned Cassiopeia. It was the same with the villagers at Milo's party, as if they were drawing away from us at first…"

"I haven't a clue what you're talking about, Bryony."

"But you must have felt it, surely. I can't put it into words. Despite that we're on holiday and we're all having such a good time, there's a sense of melancholy around the place…" My voice trails away. My feelings over Simon apart, of course and then the worry of Father's drinking and Jake's unexpected appearance, with its subsequent effect on Daisy, made worse by the fact he's presently done a runner. Never mind the usual problems with Chloe and Max. Thinking of all this, the wonder is, I still feel this holiday is so right.

"I can't say I've noticed anything…" Edward returns, patronisingly.

"There's hardly anyone ever stays in our villa. Our party happens to be one of a chosen few. It's almost as if it's meant and Cassiopeia somehow approves…"

I know I can't be making much sense but surely Edward has some awareness of all this?

It seems not. His eyes crinkle in amusement. "I'd forgotten how fey you could be, Bryony. Don't you think you're letting your imagination run away with itself, dear girl? You should write a book…"

Our steps have slowed in time to the rhythm of this island, drawn onwards by the soft clang of the church bell, growing steadily louder, a vibrating pulse impossible to ignore, calling to a place deep in my soul. I'm not sure it's struck Edward. We've reached the turning into the village and the rough square at its centre, where high days and holidays, the villagers congregate and wherein is housed the simple, white-washed stone building, with its single bell-tower, belonging to the church. A simple place of worship for uncomplicated, beautiful people.

Edward doesn't believe me and has no idea what I'm talking about. There's no point going on about it. I try to concentrate on the occasion instead and towards which, I'm discovering an increasing curiosity. Will I enjoy this service? Will it convert me to a religion; I strive and fail to understand?

We follow a steady trickle of villagers inside the porch, plunged into the cool depths of the church, with its dim, incense-filled interior, a tiny, sanctified place of worship, presently glowing with candle-light and soft shadows, sifting through a single, stained-glass window above a surprisingly elaborate fresco on the inner wall. A nave, altar and wooden chairs upon which the congregation sit, mothers and children and gnarled old fishermen, next to saintly elderly ladies, dressed all in black, all sitting with expectant, bright faces, full of hope. I wish I felt their belief too and almost, here, in such a place, I could find it in my heart to believe there really is a deity watching over us and keeping us safe.

We find a seat and sit down. Agatha and Milo arrive, and Tomas and Spiro and other strangely familiar faces I can't yet place and yet whom I remember with great clarity. My anxieties drift away. Agatha sees us and smiles and waves. At last, amongst a hum of excitement, the priest himself appears, a young man with a soft, downy face and upon whose strong, young arm, Father Ignatius leans, hobbling towards an empty chair, reserved on the front row, in which the young man sees him comfortably seated before making his way to the altar.

The service begins. Prayers, chanting and singing follow, interspersed with incomprehensible Greek from the priest, to which the congregation listens with a rapt attention, a pattern I sense set through generations. Despite the sense of exclusion this engenders, I don't, deep down, feel excluded. There's a strength to the priest's voice, to which I respond on so unconscious a level, it only deepens what I feel, that is, a burgeoning sense that here, if only I'd wits to understand it, is a simple truth.

In so short a space of time, it's over and we're following the congregation outside, into the searing heat, to stand blinking amongst the press of happy, smiling faces milling around, all apparently pleased of our presence here. Gone are the feelings of disquiet occasioned by Milo's party. We've passed a test and have been accepted here.

The bent, stick-thin figure of Father Ignatius, hobbles towards us.

"Let me offer you a little refreshment," he invites, taking my arm.

There's nothing to do but agree, besides, I'm intrigued. We pass quickly through the crowd and, skirting the outside walls of the church, we come to a narrow, dusty path between the gravestones, leading us to a flat roofed, pastel-pink villa beyond. At its door is a smiling, middle-aged woman, her hair scraped up into a bun, tied with black ribbon. She's wearing a snow-white pinafore and her hands are knotted and reddened with work. The housekeeper, I presume for she has an air of too much to do and not enough time to do it in.

With a volley of incomprehensible Greek, she ushers us inside, through a hallway, into a room furnished with simple, wooden chairs and a table and dominated by a picture of the Christ figure on one wall, underneath which she bids us sit before bringing us strong Greek coffee in tiny cups.

Father Ignatius smiles upon us benignly.

"You are troubled, my daughter..." he tells me. Perhaps he read it in my face when Agatha introduced us. I can hardly disagree, for if the church service has soothed me, inside, I'm a mass of unanswered and unanswerable questions. He sits patiently waiting, a bent, black old crow with ruffled feathers, his coffee cooling on the table at his side, his hands, paper-thin and trembling, folded together in his lap. I sip my coffee, unsure what to say or how to start. I am troubled about Cassiopeia. I'm troubled about many things, a natural born worrier me, a force of nature over which I have no control.

"Do you know the history of Cassiopeia, Father?" I ask, at last, doing my best to ignore Edward's snort of disapproval. A faint smile crosses the old man's face and he leans forward, his hands, with their long, bony fingers, steepling under his chin.

"Like all old houses, Cassiopeia has history..." he tells me and then he pauses, a growing silence in which I begin to wonder if, worn out by the morning's activities, he's dropped to sleep.

He's only marshalling his thoughts. "Cassiopeia was built two centuries ago, by a man called Drachmann," he begins. "A Jew of Italian extract, who moved his wife and son here to escape persecution, the general lot of Jews throughout the world, unfortunately. Through sound investment, his money was assured and his family prospered here, so taken into the hearts of the local people that when Drachmann's son grew into a man and he fell in love with a local girl, he married her. The young couple settled down in Cassiopeia and in due course of time, had a son of their own. This son, too, grew up to marry a local girl, so, before long, it was as if the family were truly islanders and their history here, stretching back into antiquity.

Until the arrival of Stefan, the last son of the house of Cassiopeia who, unlike any before him, was a man born with wandering feet and a burning ambition to travel and see the world. To the despair of his elderly parents, he refused to settle down and spent his youth and middle age travelling America and Europe, wherever he wished to go. When his parents died, the family name all but died with them and if only Stefan had cared! He grew old and still he travelled. He travelled until he grew infirm and crippled with arthritis.

It was the 1930s. Europe was on the brink of war and given his Jewishness, a religion to which his family had always strictly adhered, he was forced to return to Paxos and to safety. The Drachmanns had always kept contact with the various branches of their family scattered throughout Europe, some even in Nazi Germany. They were desperate times and a young daughter of the German Drachmanns, by the name of Lillie, was smuggled out of Berlin to safety, making her way, by a series of safe houses, here to Paxos and to Cassiopeia." Pausing to drink his coffee, the old man smiles. "What could Stefan do? They weren't closely related and perhaps, for more reasons than to keep her safe, he married her, astounding all who knew him. He must have been lonely. He must have seen it as his last chance to fulfil his parents' wishes for him to uphold the family name…"

"But he was an old man!" I blurt out. Edward frowns at me to keep quiet.

Father Ignatius lifts his thin shoulders.

"He was old, she was young. Local gossip had it, his great wealth softened much of the blow. And that should be the end of the story, but for the war which refused to go away, even here, in Paxos."

"The Italians occupied the Island, of course…"

Father Ignatius nods his bird-like head. "After the defeat of our armies in the Axis Balkan Campaign, Greece was occupied and our country divided between Germany, Bulgaria and Italy. Parcelled up and doled out like so much flotsam! Two thirds of Greece was occupied by Italy, with the Ionian Islands, directly administered as Italian territories…"

"That must have been hard to take," Edward intercedes.

Father Ignatius bows his head. "The Italian army in Greece as an occupying power is treated by some revisionist historians as a 'friendly force'. But the truth is, from the first days of the occupation, the Italians proceeded to cut the Islands off from Greece, a policy aimed at their annexation to Italy. Learning the Italian language became compulsory and the teaching of Greek history was restricted. They introduced a new currency and established the so-called 'Anonymous Society of Ionic Commerce' which had exclusive rights to all trade. They opened camps for 'disobedient' Greeks. There was one here, even in Paxos, a place where our people were tortured and executed…"

"But that's dreadful…"

"And what about Lillie and Stefan?" I demand, shocked at all he's told us.

"Lillie was unhappy by all accounts and not just because of the war…"

This is something I can understand. Losing her family, torn from her home and forced to marry a man so much older and so infirm. What young woman wouldn't have been unhappy? I sense there's more to come. "And, Father…" I prompt.

The elderly cleric's voice takes on a hint of disapproval. "There was a young Italian soldier, Pascal Romano, part of the occupational forces stationed in Gaius. Not a bad boy and certainly no soldier but like many, dragged into the war because that's what wars do. He was lonely, far from home…"

"And Lillie was lonely, too?" I finish for him and with a glimmer of understanding where this story might be leading.

"What hope had Stefan, an old man with nothing to offer but his wealth? Lillie and Pascal were young, they fell in love, a happening they tried to keep secret. But as ever, these secrets have a habit of getting out. The islanders, who loved Stefan, were outraged. Someone must have told him or he found out for himself. I can only imagine his despair…"

"Love is a very powerful emotion," I protest, my sympathy firmly with Lillie. "Stefan should never have married her. Whatever did he do?"

"He confronted her and because, I think, she was basically an honest girl, she confessed. When she refused to give her lover up, he complained to the Italian Commander here, a good, family man who was outraged, too. Lillie and Pascal were torn apart and there was nothing either could do. They were in the wrong and should never have fallen in love."

"Poor Lillie, poor Pascal…"

"Pascal was on the point of being sent home, back to Italy in disgrace, but then another catastrophe occurred, a happening with serious consequences for many ordinary lives…" The elderly cleric sits back and sighs. Though he could only have been a boy, that it was a bad time for him, I also sense. "It was 1943," he went on, "and the Italian forces capitulated to the Allies, in consequence of which, the Italian zone was taken over by the German army. It was a time of great confusion. Some of the Italian troops in the occupied Balkans and Greek Islands fought back but lacking any determined support by Allied forces, by the end of September, they were overwhelmed.

Seizing their chance in all the turmoil, Lillie and Pascal had secretly reunited and were on the point of eloping. Pascal stole a motorcycle and hid it in the grounds of Cassiopeia…"

"But I've seen it, Father!" I break in eagerly. He smiles gently and continues his tale.

"They had every intention of getting away to the north of the island, where they meant to bribe a fisherman to take them to the mainland. But they'd left it too late. The Germans arrived and the Italian soldiers were rounded up, Pascal amongst them and put aboard a ship destined for the mainland. In Cephalonia and Kos, Italian soldiers were simply shot. They were lucky but then…not so lucky. The Ionian was heavily mined and once out at sea, the ship, Pascal's ship, hit a mine and sank. All on board were lost, poor Pascal amongst them. Some say it was his just desserts but he was just a boy who loved, caught up in a war he didn't want or understand. He didn't deserve his end."

"Poor Lillie," I breathe and wrapped up in this story I had not expected to hear. "But what a tragedy! What happened next? Did Stefan and Lillie resolve their differences?"

Father Ignatius shakes his head. "Lillie was distraught, inconsolable, part having to hide her distress from Stefan who, a sensitive, clever man, knew it anyway. But there was worse trouble even than this. The German Army was now in total control and ordered the Islanders to give up their Jews, an order they refused. Hoping to save him, an old family friend took Stefan in, Lillie, too and did his very best to hide them – as if they had never existed! It was no good. Soldiers came and the pair were on the point of discovery when Stefan stepped out and gave himself up, swearing he was alone. I don't know why the soldiers believed him but they did. They took him away, leaving Lillie, still in hiding."

"He saved her. He must have loved her…" Edward murmurs.

"He saved her, proving by his actions that he loved her, more than life itself," Father Ignatius agrees.

"What happened to him, Father?"

"He was taken away, sent with the other Jews to Auschwitz," he concludes, grimly.

The fate of the Jews, the deepest, most terrible secret of the war. "And what happened to Lillie?" I ask, still thinking of poor Stefan and what a terrible ending for him and for so many Jews.

"Luck was with Lillie. She was smuggled away to the Greek mainland where she could more easily hide… And then my child…who knows? Only God who sees all. She simply disappeared, swallowed up by the war and no one has ever heard of her since. Her lover dead, her husband taken away, who could guess her state of mind." The elderly priest leans forward, fixing me with a stare from his rheumy eyes. "It is a mystery and the tragedy of Cassiopeia…"

# Chapter Eight

Father plonks on his panama, bids me a cheery goodbye and disappears serenely out of the door, leaving me pondering on the likelihood of my ever clapping eyes on him again. He's taking the bus into Lakka, which given all I've learned from Agatha, who is always pleased to fill me in on the details of island life, may arrive at its destination or not, depending on the whim of the driver and the day's route. Scenic or coastal? Short or convoluted? Perhaps a passenger has demanded a destination off piste, as it were and set the bus trundling off in a different direction altogether.

I pray Father won't end up off-piste. I understand he's bored. I understand, independent soul that he is, he can't bear to be stuck in the villa all day or be an encumbrance on anyone else feeling duty bound to take him out. What state he'll be in when he returns, heaven alone knows but such is life.

Having determined on a Greek salad, to be eaten as and when required, I'm at the kitchen table, venting my frustrations in chopping tomatoes and cucumber and mixing them with feta cheese and big, fat, black olives from the fridge. Chloe and Max have relented and taken Daisy to the beach. Edward and Simon have taken the car into Gaius and even now, Simon might be opening his heart to Edward about his true inclinations.

I can't bear to think of how Edward's likely to react. He'll be shocked I expect and it's a mercy he knows nothing about how close Simon and I came to betraying him. I shouldn't dwell on the history of

Cassiopeia as revealed to us by Father Ignatius, information throwing up as many imponderables as it's solved. Poor Lillie and Pascal and poor Stefan, too, marrying a girl young enough to be his daughter and then, for love of her, bravely sacrificing his life. Most of all, I wonder if Lillie's still alive and if so, where she's living. But why did she never return to Cassiopeia, after the war? Given that the islanders were upset at her affair with Pascal, probably blaming her for Stefan's death, I've no illusions concerning the reception she would have received. She might have left Greek soil altogether and travelled home to Berlin, painful as that would have been with no one in the family left to greet her. No wonder the villagers shrink at mention of Cassiopeia, a place haunted by its past. How frustrating I have no idea who owns it now, nor am I ever likely to find out. Did Stefan make a will, leaving all his worldly goods to Lillie or had he other plans? Why does no one know, or is it that they do know but aren't prepared to tell me?

My head is pounding with questions nothing to do with me and that's ironic when I'm here on holiday to relax. But I feel it in my bones. We're meant to be here in this beautiful, tranquil Greek villa. A villa with a mystery about it requiring exposure to fresh air – if only I knew what that mystery was!

With no outlet for my musings and no likelihood of any family member appearing to discuss it with, I pack a picnic of bread, boiled eggs and some of the salad and take a leisurely stroll along the narrow path hugging the hill-side, to the beach, greeted by my offspring's joyful cries, winging towards me like bird song.

Chloe and Daisy are splashing about on the edge of the waves, daring each other to venture in, whilst like the small boy he once was, Max sits cross-legged, on a rock above them, skimming stones into water clear as glass and darting with tiny rainbow-coloured fishes. They fall ravenously upon the food and like any normal family for once, we spend a leisurely hour together, talking of this and that, the first nonsense that enters our heads. Daisy shows me the shells she's collected. I've half a mind to talk to Max about Edward and to Chloe about school and university but why spoil the moment? England is so far away, its problems belonging to another family, a fractious, self-opinionated body I'm becoming increasingly loathe to resurrect. Given time and distance, Chloe will surely see reason about her future, whilst Max is already settling back into a normal relationship with Edward. My older children are happy, embarking upon their first, tentative adult relationships, whilst Daisy appears to have forgotten her father's non-appearance.

I leave them to it, and dawdle back to the villa, where I pour myself a well-deserved glass of wine and finding a shadier part of the terrace, sit down with a book so that soon, the morning's concerns over Cassiopeia slide away into nothingness.

"Oh, God, Bryony…"

I open one eye and squint up at Simon, for of course it is he, alerted by his expression that his intimate lunch with Edward might not have gone to plan. He looks hot and bothered and worse, stressed out of his complacency.

"Where's Edward?"

"Still in Gaius. I've walked back and I hope to God he does, too because he's in no fit state to drive…"

"Are you two okay?" Stupid question when it's perfectly clear they're not. Simon seizes the bottle of wine from the table and topping up my glass, takes a hefty swig.

He breathes in deeply.

"No, we're not," he answers me.

"He wasn't happy with what you've told him?" I prompt, stifling the urge to shake him. Why are men so obtuse when it comes to discussing their feelings? Simon takes another swig of wine, then throws himself down into a chair, cradling his glass between his hands and staring hopelessly into its depths.

"He accused me of stringing him along," he tells me, sorrowfully, looking up at last. "That I've been pretending to be someone I'm not. I suppose he has a point…"

"You told him you're attracted to women?"

"After a fashion…"

"Well, did you, or didn't you?"

"Yes, of course I did."

"And that you don't want to miss out on family life?"

"That, too. I thought he'd understand… The conversation got heated."

This doesn't sound like the Edward I know and love, normally the most approachable of men.

There's something else, too, something Simon isn't telling me.

"And?" I prompt.

"And, nothing…" he says, evasively. "Only…"

"Only what, Simon?" I demand, instinct telling me I might not like what I'm about to hear.

"Like I said, the conversation got heated. I must admit, a crowded restaurant was hardly the time or place. We said a lot of stuff we'd probably have been better keeping to ourselves…"

A dim suspicion raises its head. "Simon… You didn't tell him about us?"

Of course, there is no 'us'. The words are clutched out of thin air, a nightmare scenario.

"Well…not exactly…"

"Well did you, or didn't you?"

"It was when he said he'd have been better off stopping with you and holding you up as some kind of paragon from which I fell far short. We'd both had a fair bit to drink by then."

"What the hell did you say to him? Tell me – I want to know every word!"

"I said that I was attracted to you," he mumbles, wretchedly but if that sounds bad enough to my ears, there's even worse to follow. "I told him…that you were attracted to me, too."

"Oh, God, Simon, you didn't…"

"I'd have taken it back if I could but he stormed off and never gave me chance. I last saw him sitting in a bar on the waterfront, knocking back whisky like nobody's business. I thought it best to leave him."

"I can't believe what a mess you've made..."

"I told him a kiss was as far as it went…"

I make a grab for the wine and drink deeply. There's nothing I can say or do that will rectify this catastrophe. A kiss is a kiss and the one Simon and I shared was far from innocent. Whatever must Edward be thinking? The man with whom he wants to spend the rest of his life, turns out to be someone other than whom he thought, whilst the woman who was once his wife, the mother of his children, has betrayed him in the very worst way possible. He must feel as if his world's fallen apart and when this holiday was meant to put his life back together again.

"I'd better go to him!" I cry, springing up.

If I don't love Edward in a physical way anymore, then I love him like the big brother I've always wanted. I can't bear to think of him in pain and that I'm to blame. Which would be quickest? To run into the village, to the shop, to ask Agatha to take me into Gaius, with the bonus, I'd have help getting him home? Given Boadicea's disinclination to go anywhere in a hurry, it might be just as quick to walk and if he really is drunk, it's probably better Agatha has nothing to do with it. There's a strong streak of morality in these islanders and she might think badly of him.

I hope Edward's not too drunk. I hope he's not belligerent. I hope I can find him.

My head is all over the place. Simon retrieves the wine glass back and drains it.

"Are you coming with me?" I demand.

"I've only come back to pack. I thought it best to clear off and lie low a while. I'll try the hotel in Gaius, just for a day or two, until he's calmed down."

In other words, it doesn't matter how badly Edward's feeling, just so long as he's not allowed to vent his spleen on Simon who deserves it – as do I, I remind myself. It must have been some argument. In high dudgeon, wondering now, stunning good looks and bags of sex appeal apart, whatever it was that I saw in Simon, I stalk off, making my way towards Gaius, via the short cut along the beach and taking the opportunity to both check on the children and to ensure that Max and Chloe will keep an eye on Daisy whilst I'm gone. I might be a bad parent but I've not totally absolved my responsibilities yet.

"I want to come too, Mummy…" Daisy protests, at once, as I knew she would.

"I'm not stopping, Darling. I'll be back before you know it…"

"What's up, Mum?" Max asks quietly and sensitive as ever.

"Nothing…that is…I just need you to keep an eye on Daisy."

They know something's up, they're not daft, even Daisy who exhibits a maturity beyond her age.

Appallingly, given who her father is, she's used to trouble. Aware I'm not making much sense and for Edward's sake, not wishing to answer any more questions, I hurry away, for once uncaring of the glorious lushness of the countryside I pass through and yet the sights and sounds and tantalizing perfumes of which subconsciously invade my every senses. I need to find Edward, if only to assure him that…what? I didn't make a pass at his boyfriend? It was all a huge mistake I'll regret until the day I die? I did make a pass and there's no getting away from it. I still can't believe Simon's told him.

Given it's the Sabbath, the town is wearing a subdued air and even the tourists, mindful of local sensitivity, pay their respects by presenting a serene demeanour. A quick search of the waterfront cafes, many of which are shutting for the afternoon siesta, fails to turn up sight or sound of Edward. I'm dreading to find him for I haven't a clue what to say to repair the damage I've caused. I can't see him in the square, nor in any of the numerous streets leading from it, though that doesn't signify that he's not there, merely that I can't be everywhere at once. I must look troubled for I receive many curious looks.

And then, after long minutes fruitless searching, I have a brainwave. After all he's supposedly drunk, I can't imagine he'll be thinking of driving back to Cassiopeia but he may well have returned to the car to sleep it off. The town's car parks might be a good place to start.

I can count the times I've seen Edward drunk on the fingers of one hand. He wouldn't drive…would he, not when he's always been so law-abiding and sensible? I have no idea of Greek drink driving laws but I know for sure they have some in place and that it's asking for trouble to go beyond their limits. I begin another search, systematically this time, of all the car-parks, fruitlessly as it turns out but then, just when I've given up hope, miraculously, I see him. There's what can only loosely be described as a car park across from 'Spiro's', one of the more popular supermarkets in town, a derelict tarmacked area, covered with weeds. Today, there's only a smattering of customers' cars parked and thus my gaze comes easily to rest on a mustard-coloured Renault, surely our hire car, a swaying figure by its side, confirming it. It's Edward, red-faced and dishevelled, signs worryingly suggesting his state of intoxication. With a mixture of joy and a growing horror, I hurry towards him. He's attempting to put the key in the door, a manoeuvre in which, thankfully, he's having little success.

"Edward..." I reach out a tentative hand to take the keys but perceiving my intent, peevishly he snatches them away, cradling them closely to his chest. He swears under his breath and in another bid to fit the key into the lock, sways forward, this time and by some miracle, achieving his aim. He turns the key and the door swings open and seeing him about to get inside, in the vain hope of delaying him, I seize hold of his arm.

"Edward, please..."

"Leave me 'lone, you...you...Jezebel..." he slurs, shrugging me away.

"Edward, please, listen to me. We do need to talk but not now...later...when you're in a better frame of mind. If you're thinking of driving, you're in no fit state. Please...come with me..."

"Am goin' home," he mutters, belligerently.

"Listen to lady..." says a firm voice, in pigeon English, nearly scaring me out of my wits. The man to whom it belongs has crept up on us unawares and I see, with a sickening feeling of dread, that it's a uniformed member of the Greek Police Force,

apparently materializing out of thin air, the first
policeman I've clapped eyes on since we got here –
and now of all times! I'd no idea such a body existed
in virtually crime free Paxos but I vaguely remember
seeing a police station marked when I studied the map
of Gaius. This particular policeman is only doing his
job and has probably been watching Edward a while.

He appears amiable enough but it's not a good
situation to find ourselves in.

"Sharn't if'n I don' wan…" Edward tells him,
with great dignity.

Deftly and with my full approval, the
policeman whips the keys out of Edward's hand.
Then turning to me with a smile, he bows and
presents them to me. He's rather sweet, I think and if
he's still wet behind the ears, he is attractive, in a
rugged kind of way. There's no mistaking the gleam
in his eyes, or the way his gaze holds mine just that
fraction too long. He likes me and I like him too, I
think, longingly, my only excuse being, I'm
unaccustomed to all this heat and relentless sunshine
and it's gone to my head. Greek men like looking at
women, of any nationality and I'm in sore need of
masculine approval. Heaven forbid Edward's right,
I'm at such a low ebb in my life, romantically
speaking, that is, I'm behaving like the Jezebel to
which he's likened me. All the same, another day, in
different circumstances, who knows…

I take myself to task. Edward isn't going to
take this interference lying down and I'm
remembering now, too late, that on one of those very
few occasions I have seen him the worse for wear, he
was surprisingly belligerent and all over some minor

matter in Chambers with which he disagreed. His stream of invective when Father refused, finally, to back down, shocked us all. It was at a Chambers Christmas party when matters came to a head and unfortunately, there were a lot of the firm's clients present. Edward apologised in the morning, when he'd sobered up, of course and considering at the time he was the heir to the family business, the man ready to step into Father's considerable shoes, Father accepted it and no more was said.

Edward and drink simply don't mix. Before I can stop him, he snatches the keys back and in the ensuing scuffle, the policeman's hat is knocked to the floor. It might have been my fault but the policeman appears to think it's Edward's. Pouring oil on the flames, Edward starts to laugh.

"Hah!" he crows, triumphantly.

At once, the atmosphere becomes charged. Before Edward can blink, or backtrack or even apologise, any of the things he'd do by instinct if only he was sober, the policeman whips a pair of hand-cuffs out of his top pocket and has his hands pinioned behind his back.

"You come with me!" he snaps, snapping the hand-cuffs shut.

"Oh, please…you can't do that…he didn't mean it…" I gabble, if only too wretchedly aware my protests aren't making the slightest difference. Edward has been arrested. I pick up the policeman's hat from the floor, brushing it down apologetically, before handing it back. "I'm so sorry. I think I might have knocked it off. Edward's entirely innocent," I implore.

Whether he is or not, it's too late. Pausing only to return his hat to his head, the policeman seizes his arm and begins to lead him away. It's amazing how quickly one can sober up when faced with catastrophe. After his false show of bravado, unsurprisingly, Edward now looks sick and scared. I'm scared, too. The Greek judiciary system is not like ours; their police force is part of their military structure. Goodness knows what's going to happen to him now.

"Can I help?" enquires a wonderfully familiar voice.

Amazingly, of all people, it's Jake and for once in his life, I'm desperately pleased to see him. I've no idea where he's been hiding since he ran off and left Daisy and I to the tender mercies of the British press, but quite simply, at this moment, I couldn't care less.

"Jake…thank God you're here…Edward…this policeman… he's been arrested…" I gabble incoherently.

"Please move out of way…" The policeman states, imperiously. Jake is blocking his path and he regards him coldly before, most oddly and exactly as if someone has waved a magic wand and produced a miracle, his whole manner changes. His belligerence fades and a wondering look crosses his face. "You are…yes! Tell me you are! Wembley…two years since…you play for United and score winning goal…it is…Mr…Jake Turnbull!"

"Yep, that's me," Jake agrees, modestly.

It's the policeman's turn to gabble and he's wonderfully servile, even more so than me, in my ham-fisted attempt to set Edward free. "Is wonderful goal!" he beams. "I on holiday on mainland, visiting parents. The match beamed back live. We always watch the English cup. I play a little myself, you know…" he concludes, smugly.

"It was a shame you couldn't have been there in person," Jake murmurs, pleasantly. He leans forward, smiling confidentially. "That is… I could always get you a couple of complimentary tickets for the next England match. It's always good to meet a fellow footballer…"

The man is putty in his hands. Before I know it, a name and address has been punched into Jake's phone, Edward is released, the keys handed politely back to me, which I immediately stuff into my bag out of harm's way. With a stern caution to Edward, the policeman salutes Jake smartly before strolling away, exactly as if nothing has happened and no offence whatsoever has occurred. A miracle has been achieved and by Jake, of all people. And thank God for him, I realise, something I never thought to find myself thinking. Edward grins inanely at the policeman's retreating back. I've no idea how much he's had to drink but far more than he's used too. His gaze locks on mine and his smile slides away.

"Jezebel," he hisses.

I'm not to be forgiven, then. Jake's cool gaze fills with a dancing amusement, instantly undoing my good feelings towards him. "We'd better get him home," he drawls. "What about Edward's car?"

"There's only Edward insured to drive it…"

"Wait here and don't let him wander off. I'll find us a taxi…"

In an incredibly short space of time, he's back, hopping out of the taxi-cab he's brought with him, helping me into the back with Edward, smoothing the situation over with the driver with promises of extra cash. As soon as we're seated, Edward's head inclines onto my shoulder and he promptly and thankfully falls asleep. His snores accompany our journey.

Wearily, I accept I couldn't have managed without Jake, hardly my ideal of a knight in shining armour. Our luck holds because back at Cassiopeia, though Father has returned, he's sprawled asleep over the paper and the children, back from the beach, are otherwise occupied, scavenging for food in the kitchen. Thankfully, there's no sign of Simon. Simon would only complicate matters. Between us, Jake and I manage to smuggle Edward inside, up the stairs to his room, where we get him to bed and leave him to sleep it off. He's going to have one hell of a hangover.

True to form, Jake is enjoying my discomfort. "The demon drink…" he goads, once we're back downstairs again. By common consent, we've returned to the terrace, relieved to find Father still asleep and snoring like a baby.

"It wasn't my fault," I return, heatedly and thinking of Simon who at this precise moment, I'd rather like to boil in a vat of oil. Painful as leaving him would be, in the initial stages at least, I'm beginning to think Edward would be better off without him. But this isn't Simon, it's Jake and Jake and I have history of our own. As always, attack is the best form of defence. "And anyway, where the hell have you been? You had no business abandoning me and Daisy…"

"I had no choice. I've been holed up in Lakka, out of harm's way," he returns, baldly.

The bottle of wine is still open on the table and I'm relieved to see by its level, Father can only have helped himself to a single glass. Jake disappears to find a couple of clean glasses, returning with a garrulous Daisy in tow, from which point, the rest of the day takes care of itself. Unsurprisingly, she clings to her father like a limpet. With much shouting and banging of doors, Chloe and Max make themselves ready and head off to Gaius where they're planning a meal and a late night with Milo and Alex, at Alex's place of work. They appear unsurprised to see Jake back but then, he's always had a habit of turning up unexpectedly. Woken by Daisy's excited prattle, Father regales us with tales of a hair-raising bus-ride into Lakka and of an even more hair-raising taxi-journey back.

I disappear into the kitchen where I retrieve the Greek salad from the fridge, find fruit and bread and open a fresh bottle of wine. We sit round the table together, the meal dominated by Daisy's chatter, to which the adults listen with a resigned air. Is Jake staying or is this a temporary blip? I wish he'd go home, back to England to sort his life out.

"Come on, Daisy, let's do the washing-up," he proffers ingratiatingly, after we've eaten and no doubt attempting to make up for running out on us yesterday. With a happy giggle, Daisy springs up and rushes after him, a little bird, hopping after its parent, desperate for crumbs of affection and if only he could see what he's doing to her. I admit he's always been good with her, when he bothers to put himself out that is. Her laughter drifts up towards us, onto the terrace.

I've explained Edward's absence to Father as caused by one of the bad heads to which he's always been prone, whilst Simon's disappearance I put down to a spot of sight-seeing. Father appears to accept it though he regards me curiously and I wonder if I've fooled him.

"I bought a paper in Lakka. I've been meaning to show you this, when we had a moment alone," he murmurs, handing his paper over and watching me frowningly as I take in the photograph splashed across its front pages. Thank the heavens, they've obscured Daisy's face but there we all are, sitting round the table in Gaius, the lurid headlines suggesting I'm Jake's latest squeeze.

"Has Jake seen it?" I explode.

"I expect so," Father answers. He's never liked Jake, rightly thinking I could have done so much better. Father never thinks anyone's good enough for me but that Jake's dragged Daisy into his shady going-ons, is clearly unforgivable. I hide the paper, out of Daisy's sight, biting down on my temper and letting Jake put her to bed and read her a bed-time story. Tactfully, Father takes himself off early to bed. He can be tactful when he wants to be though I can see he's itching to have a go at Jake. Once Daisy's dropped off to sleep, Jake returns downstairs. Fire-flies hover on the bushes beyond the bottom terrace, tiny bright sparkles of shimmering light. Night is falling, cocooning us in warmth and healing my temper.

"I suppose you've seen the paper?" I hiss.

"Ahhh…."

"Is that all you have to say?"

"Sorry," he says, unexpectedly. He pours us the last of the wine, then taking his drink, leans back against the trellis, separating the top terrace from the one below. "I didn't ask the papers to follow me over here, Bryony…"

"But you might have known they would."

"It's like living in a blasted goldfish bowl. I've had enough…"

"I thought you loved football?"

"I can't imagine my life without it but given the short lifespan of your average footballer, I'm going to have too, soon. I want to make the most of the little time I have left of my playing career but I can't stand the baggage that comes along with it nowadays…"

"It's brought you an incredible life-style," I point out, reasonably. Most people would give their all to live Jake's life. Lucrative advertising contracts requiring little or no effort on his behalf, always the best seats in the restaurant and fawning adulation from the fans, all for a little early morning training and a match or two thrown in along the way. The rest of his time is his to spend as he pleases.

Rich he's complaining about it now.

"And I'm grateful for it," he protests. "Look…do you mind? Can't we talk about something else? What about you? What made you drag the family here, of all places? Someone said you'd sold your business?"

Normally, Jake's main topic of conversation is himself and the fact he wants to talk about me, sets an amazing precedent. But after the kind of day I've had, I need to talk and talking to Jake, who knows all about me, is surprisingly easy. Bucking the trend of a life-time, I find myself telling him my worries over Father and the over-riding desire to get away from England that brought us here, even, thoughtlessly, broaching on the mess I'm currently making of my life. Mikey, the business, the trouble with the children and not knowing where or who to turn to next. Then I touch on Edward and Simon's relationship, watching his face warily for the slightest trace of amusement, surprised at its absence.

"It just feels right, being here at Cassiopeia. As if it was meant," I go on. "Don't you feel that, too – that there's something special about this place?" Jake doesn't say anything to this and entirely unprovoked, I find myself recounting Father Ignatius' tale concerning Pascal and Lillie and of Stefan Drachmann and the tragedy of the war, a tragedy that lingers still and haunts this place, I'm sure of it. I'm sensitive, I pick up on vibes, I don't need evidence, I just know it. Does any of this make sense?

And then, just when we're getting on, in a way we haven't for years, Jake has to spoil it.

"Haunting? Vibes? You'll be saying you've seen a ghost next," he goads, with such a smug smile, instantly, I want to slap him.

But I have seen a ghost and I'm only thankful I haven't said so. The ghost of a girl that I thought was Chloe and yet wasn't Chloe. A mere trick of the light or a part of Cassiopeia's history sent to haunt me? Either way, it's made me long to find out more. Typical Jake, leading me on, making me think there's a decent human being in there somewhere, lurking under all the pretence. I put down my glass with a flourish.

"Go to hell, Jake Turnbull," I say and then, seeing him flinch, instantly, I'm ashamed of myself.

But this means too much to me and Jake can think what he likes. There is something odd, here at Cassiopeia. I'm surer than ever that our presence here is meant and whether Jake scoffs or not, I mean to find out why that is.

## Chapter Nine

"She walks in beauty, like the night, of cloudless climes and starry skies…"
Being sober hasn't curtailed Father's outbursts, albeit Byron is hard to take this time in the morning.

"Good morning, Father."

"My love…" he beams, pouring me coffee, finding me bread, honey and fruit juice from the wreck of the breakfast table. Daisy's laughter drifts up from the terrace below. She's playing softball with Jake, fortunately having inherited her athletic abilities from her father rather than her mother, who hates sporting activity of any kind. Jake's playing the role of doting father to a tee and, half asleep as I am, I wonder, what's in it for him? I suspect he's trying to make up for running out on us in Gaius but that would suggest he has a conscience. More likely, he's lying low until the press pack give up trying to find him. Then we shall see his true metal. Poor Daisy. I won't let him hurt Daisy.

"You're looking well, Father. This holiday is doing you good," I observe, dragging my mind back to the sticking point. Father is sober and has been since our little chat. I'm proud of him.

"It is doing me good," he agrees, heartily. "And you, my love?"

"And me, what?"

He regards me pityingly but what can he expect this time in the morning? I've slept well, too well, in fact and my brain is sluggish, still caught up with the events of yesterday. Edward and the policeman and the fact Edward now knows I fancy Simon and that worse, Simon fancies me.

"Is this holiday doing you good?" he repeats patiently, patience and Father being two words I wouldn't normally link together.

"I think so," I answer, suddenly unsure. Jake's arrival, the thorn in the tender rose of Paxos life, has complicated matters. I've no idea what to do about Edward and Simon, nor my fixation with this villa and its shady past.

Chloe stumbles onto the terrace. She looks a wreck, I observe, with my critical mother's eye. Miraculously, she finds herself a clean cup from amongst the debris and pours herself a coffee, which she takes black, no sugar. Thankfully, there's no sign of her father yet, nor her brother either, whom I assume has already breakfasted, having caught a glimpse of him earlier, out of my bedroom-window, hurrying beach-wards, his guitar slung across his back. I swear he's welded to it. Arriving home in the early hours, out at the crack of dawn, or what passes for dawn on this sleepy island, I imagine he's taken the short cut into Gaius, to spend the day with Alex. What it is to be young and in love! I can hardly remember either. Chloe sits huddled into herself, sipping her coffee, declining her Grandfather's offer of breakfast, with a morose shake of her head.

"Some fruit then," he persists.

"I'm not hungry."

"You have to eat," he admonishes.

"Is everything alright?" I ask, though it's patently clear it's not. She must have fallen out with Milo.

"How's Milo?" Father demands, tactlessly, her petulant shrug to this confirming my suspicions.

"Would you like to talk about it?" I suggest, tentatively, amazed to be taken up on the offer.

"You'd better ask Agatha…" she begins, belligerently.

"What's Agatha done?"

"You know Milo's going to Athens in the autumn, to study photography at the School of Fine Art…"

"I didn't, actually…"

"He's very good. I've seen his work…"

I've seen him with a camera slung around his neck but it's never crossed my mind he's intending to turn it into a profession, a very lucrative profession, I should imagine, if he's as good as Chloe suggests.

"Well, no wonder Agatha's so proud of him…" I suggest, daringly.

"Hah! We all know Greek mothers and their sons…"

"Please, Chloe, tell me, what's wrong?"

She's quivering with indignation. "Athens' is fine with me, of course it is. I knew from the start that was where he was headed at the end of the summer. But Agatha thinks I'm distracting him, taking his mind from his studies…"

"She might have a point, love…" There's a split second when I think, I can't believe I've just said that, adding oil to the fire, throwing paraffin onto rampant flames and standing back to watch the conflagration. Tact has never been my strong point either. Unfortunately, Father brought me up to speak my mind and I throw him a troubled glance, wishing instead, he'd taught me to think before I open my big, fat mouth. Some people would say our whole family is too opinionated by far.

"Hah! I might have known whose side you'd be on!" she snorts.

"She probably only means you should cool things a little, Darling…"

"Do you think I'd be in this state if that was all it was?" she yells at me. "She's only arranged for him to stay with his Uncle, in Athens. Acclimatise himself to the city before Uni, she says and earn himself some money into the bargain, by working in the family taxi business. There's a vacancy, apparently, very conveniently and she wants him to go today, tomorrow by the latest…"

"Oh dear."

"Is that all you can say? Oh dear!" This last is delivered in the scathing tones my daughter reserves for times of great tribulation – which happens far too often, in my opinion. I don't know what to say. It's too late, in any case, for she's leapt up and pausing only to throw me a withering look, she flounces off, heading quickly away from the villa. I make to follow her but Father lays a restraining hand on my arm.

"Leave her, my love. You two are like fire and water. I'll go," he finishes grandly. Brimming with the self-belief he can make a better job of helping her than me, her mother, he heaves himself to his feet and heads off after her. Another family trait is an unswerving belief in our own abilities, only unfortunately, it's by-passed me entirely. I can never do anything right.

Poor Chloe and poor Milo, too, I think, making a desultory start on the clearing up. I wonder where those two young people will go from here and if that will be an end to their budding romance. Should I have done more to persuade them to cool things a while? I pray Father will help Chloe to see it from Agatha's point of view. Agatha, who has brought Milo up, virtually single-handed and by all accounts, made a wonderful job of it. Naturally, she's worried for his future and determined nothing should get in the way of her ambitions for him, her only child. Unfortunately, in the process, she's hurt Chloe, for which I'm burning to give her a piece of my mind.

Jake and Daisy join us.

"Daddy and I are going to look for shells!" Daisy crows, volleying the information at me, a fait accompli, as it were. I might have plans myself but Jake would never consider this.

"I hope that's okay?" he placates, rightly sensing an atmosphere. "What's up with Chloe? She's just shot out of here like a bat out of hell... Trouble?"

"Don't ask. Father's gone after her..."

"Why don't you come with us?" he enquires, looking surprisingly like he means it. Just for a moment, I can think of no reason why not but duty calls and Chloe might have need of me.

"I'd better wait for Father. Perhaps later? I'll catch you up," I return, equally as pleasantly.

We try for Daisy's sake and I'm relieved to see Jake making such an effort, too.

"Make sure you do," he says, disappearing into the kitchen, quickly reappearing with a haversack and heading them off towards the beach. Daisy's prattle dwindles into nothingness and the silence is bliss. The day can only get better but of course it doesn't, anything but.

"Bryony!" It seems impossible to inject so much hurt into a single name. Edward's still in his pyjamas, his haggard appearance suggesting his hangover is every bit as bad as I'd imagined. My insides do a double somersault. I've no idea what to say to him.

"How are you feeling?" I enquire, already treading on egg shells.

"How am I feeling? Absolutely fine, given I have a two-timing wretch for an ex-boyfriend and a hussy for an ex-wife…" he retorts, his voice ringing with sarcasm.

Is a hussy better or worse than a Jezebel? I take a deep breath and launch in. He deserves an apology at least and it might, conceivably, deflect some of his understandable anger.

"Edward, I am sorry. I don't know what came over me. It was only a kiss, it didn't mean anything. It was all my fault," I add, between gritted teeth, doing my best to leave the path clear for Simon, who doesn't deserve it.

"Simon says he fancies you."

"He's trying to protect me, take the blame…"

"Come off it, Bryony."

"He's confused; he doesn't know what he means…"

And neither do I, come to that, because I realise now, in the cold light of dawn, or near enough, that I still fancy him. Simon is eminently fanciable though there's no way I'll let anything physical happen between us again. Simon is strictly off-limits and I should have known that from the out-set. Edward sinks into a chair and buries his face in his hands. Full of remorse, I make fresh coffee and toast, rushing back up onto the terrace with it and sitting to watch him eat, very slowly, a little at a time. Afterwards, I'm relieved to see a little colour return to his face. At least he hasn't tried to kill me yet, though I'm not sure if that's just Edward, being Edward, such a gentle man, or his hangover is of such monumental proportions, the effort might finish him off. I pour myself a cup of coffee and sip it slowly.

"I'm lonely Edward. I think that's why it happened. I knew it was wrong but I'd had too much to drink and so had Simon. We both regret it, terribly…"

"Do you know where he is?"

"Holed up in the hotel in Gaius, giving you chance to calm down. You two need to talk."

I'm only stating the obvious. Edward glares at me. "I can't get my head round some of the stuff he told me. What I can remember that is…"

If he's forgotten about the policeman and the policeman's hat, I'm not about to remind him.

"Why don't you have a shower and get dressed. See how you're feeling afterwards. You'll have to go into Gaius to fetch the car and whilst you're about it, if you're up to it, you could always go and find Simon. The only way you two will sort this out is by talking and being honest with each other."

"He wants children. He fancies women."

"I know, he told me…"

"I don't know him anymore."

"Perhaps it's just there's more to find out than you thought. We all have hidden depths, Edward…"

And then some. Thankfully, he sees the sense of this and rises to his feet.

"I'm disappointed in you, too, Bryn," he tells me, with great dignity.

"You have every right to be," I agree and if I'm being servile, so be it. It seems to me, the best way forward. There's no point antagonizing him further, adding fuel to the fire, as it were. I've done enough of that already.

"I thought better of you."

"Of course you did."

"I'll get over it, I expect…"

And with that sage comment, he trundles off, back into the villa, leaving me staring balefully after him. I deserve to feel terrible. Poor Edward – and poor me! The only certainty is that sitting here moping won't do the slightest bit of good. There's no sign of Father or Chloe yet and I have a worrying feeling, before the situation gets any better, it might conceivably get very much worse.

This holiday has gone from calm to storm in a flash and crazily, I feel even the villa, my sanctuary, my port in any storm, is sulking quietly in the background, wondering what kind of people it has living here and what we might do next. That, as they say, is anyone's guess and perhaps mine most of all.

Finally, I get to clear the table and wash the pots, tidying up along the way and trying not to think of anything much, lulling myself, as a form of self-protection, into a state where my senses shut down. It's less painful that way. When I've finished, I wander back out, onto the terrace, wondering what I ought to do next. As usual though, on this day of all days, events take care of themselves. From the bottom terrace, a plump figure, like an angry bumblebee, hurtles up the steps towards me.

It's Agatha and she's obviously run all the way from the village because it takes her a full minute to catch her breath. She stands, wringing her hands and making strange, moaning noises.

"Where are they?" she demands, once she's in control enough to speak.

"Where are whom?" I ask, mechanically but suspicion already raising its ugly head.

"Chloe…that Chloe…"

"Chloe's with Father…"

Agatha draws herself up to her full height, which even so, is still thankfully slightly below mine.

"Father is in shop, serving… He take over from Milo when I go see Father Ignatius for blessing for Milo's visit to my brother, Demetrius, in Athens. When I come back they 'ave disappeared…"

Everything is clear to me now. Meddling as ever, Father's has relieved Milo of his duties in the shop so that Milo and Chloe will have chance to say goodbye properly. I hate to tell Agatha, knowing Father, he's probably already sold the floor from under her feet, fixtures, fittings, the lot.

"Father…he say the young ones, they need to talk…"

"Agatha, I think he might be right," I coax gently. "Even I can see how much they mean to each other. But it's just puppy love, nothing serious, you mustn't be too worried…"

"But Milo, he go to his Uncle. All is arranged! I buy ticket for Christa this afternoon," she wails.

"He 'as connection to catch in Corfu! No time to waste. He not even packed! I need to find him, double quick…"

It appears to me, act in haste and repent at leisure but given she's so worked up already, for once in charge of my motor mouth, I stifle the impulse to tell her so. "They'll be back," I soothe. "And no doubt in plenty of time. I'll return with you. It'll do me good to stretch my legs and we'll probably find them waiting when we get there…" Moreover, it'll give me a chance to check up on Father, who might be big enough and ugly enough to look after himself but who shouldn't be over-exerting himself. I can't wait to give him a piece of my mind. Causing trouble by siding with Chloe, instead of taking the long-term view, which is that Agatha has a point.

"Perhaps you're right, Agatha," I say, uncertainly. "Milo and Chloe are rather young for a steady relationship."

"They need to concentrate on study."

"Of course, they do, at their age and I'm sure they will…"

It's not up to this family to comment on Agatha's ambition for Milo, nor of her abrupt solution in sending him away. Even if it was only a holiday romance, hurting no one and surely better left to die a natural death on our return to England. I'm prepared to bet my life that's what would have happened.

"They only want to say goodbye, Agatha," I reiterate. "It's perfectly understandable…"

I'm not sure she agrees with me but we walk back towards the village together, placidly enough, meandering along the winding track between the twisted olive groves through which the sun gleams. I think, inconsequentially, how wonderful it must be to live here, a throwback to how life ought to be and sadly once was. The past in which Paxos is so charmingly rooted, and it reminds me.

"Agatha… You mentioned a woman who used to work here at Cassiopeia, the housekeeper, I think you said. Did you tell me she was still alive…?"

"Eleni Mitsopoulos, yes. She old woman now, lives with her daughter in Corfu Town, near old fort. She go away after war and work in Athens, I think. But someone say, she come home again. I mean long time to go see her, perhaps but… You know 'ow it is." She shrugs. I do know. It's called life, the distraction that gets in the way of everything we ought to do and never get around too.

"Do you think she might know who owns Cassiopeia? I'd love to know if Lillie is still alive."

Agatha stops, dead in her tracks, treating me to an odd look before crossing herself.

"It's alright," I soothe her. "Father Ignatius's told me about Stefan and Lillie and Pascal. It's a very sad tale but I still can't understand why no-one will talk to me about it. It's a big part of the history of Cassiopeia but what happened there during the war can't hurt anyone now…"

Agatha shakes her head. "Who know if Lillie still alive? No one bother to ask! Is gone, long time ago. Best not to talk. Is sad house. And sadness catch, like illness. This is what we believe…"

Island superstition again and who am I to scoff. Unexpectedly, she smiles.

"Is good you come here. Make house happy again!"

We've turned off the track and are headed into the village and I wonder why it is, I'm so pleased that despite the dysfunctional nature of our family, local perception is that our presence here is a positive force for the good. Father's certainly is. We enter the shop to find him happily ensconced behind the counter, panama pushed to the back of his head and with his sleeves rolled up, greeted by his dulcet tones holding forth to a knot of curious village women, grouped across the counter, shaking their heads and frowning at their overflowing baskets, proof of his sales technique. Father can turn his hand to anything and usually does. His confidence amazes me.

Business, it appears, has been brisk and if Agatha is still concerned about Milo catching the ferry in good time, Father's efforts on her behalf, softens her mood. Despite his treachery, my elderly parent can do no wrong in her eyes and she shoots him an adoring glance, which he bats away with great equanimity. With assurances we'll let her know immediately if Chloe and Milo turn up back at the villa, I prise him away, unsurprised by his reluctance. He's enjoyed getting back into the flow and I accept, on our return to England, he'll demand to resume the reins of his business. I won't tell him, over my dead body, but battle lines are already drawn.

"I thought you weren't keen on Agatha?"

"Merely helping out a fellow human being in need, my love."

"Everything would have been fine if only she'd left Chloe and Milo alone. Where do you think they've got to? Milo must know he'll miss the boat…"

"I only gave them a chance to talk…"

"You've no need to look so full of yourself," I snap, in a vain attempt to deflate his pomposity. "Look what trouble you've caused…"

He shrugs dismissively. We've taken refuge on the terrace and sit drinking long, ice-cold glasses of orange and lemon. The cold jolts my thought processes and I think, suddenly of Jake and Daisy and how I promised I'd go with them to the beach. I need to find them, forthwith, meanwhile keeping my eyes peeled for Chloe and Milo, who must be somewhere roundabout.

"I really need to go and check on Daisy!" I cry, springing up. "Can you keep an eye out for Chloe and Milo until I get back? I won't be long!"

"Of course, my love…" he promises eagerly, too eagerly, I realise afterwards.

I haven't got time to think. I leave him engrossed in his book, one of the lurid crime stories of which he's so inordinately fond and departing quickly, I head for the path to the beach, meanwhile enjoying the sensation of the sun dappling through the trees which shade my hurried footsteps. Paxos is a web of connecting pathways, situated in strange, unexpected places and when I reach the beach, with no sign yet of Daisy and Jake, by the mere expediency of climbing steps carved into the rock above me, I'm able to meander along a little winding path which weaves by rocky outlets and bright, unexpected bays, my steps accompanied by the soothing sound of waves.

There's not a boat in sight, nor person either and it's as if the island belongs to me and to me alone, making of me a castaway, embalmed in a great, vast solitude. The infinity of nature pitted against the insignificance of man, or woman, as it were. So deep in thought am I, pondering on this imponderable, I'm almost disappointed to find what I'm looking for, alerted to Daisy's presence by her cries, which are ear-shatteringly loud. She's happy, so much is clear, I think, catching sight of her and Jake by the water's edge. Jake is teaching her to skim stones. Posed against the blue sea, I think they might be any normal father and child and it crosses my mind to wonder if he ever regrets all he's missed of her childhood.

He turns and sees me and an odd look crosses his face.

"We'd given you up…"

"Look, Mummy, I can skim stones!"

I watch her awhile before going to sit on a low, flat rock, jutting out over the sea, unsurprised when Jake joins me. We need to talk, particularly about Daisy and particularly about his slapdash method of stop, start parenting.

"I'm pleased you're spending time with her," I say, pointedly. "She needs her father in her life."

"You've no need to tell me, Bryony," he answers, sounding cross and defensive and a lot of other things too. There are hidden agendas between us, leaving me torn between wanting what's best for Daisy, which is Jake in her life, and my desperate desire to get him out of mine and back to England.

We can't be in each other's company for five minutes without falling out. That's just the way it is and I wish it wasn't but we can't always have what we want, unfortunately.

Clasping his hands across his knees, he stares out to sea.

"We did some good with Daisy," he remarks, unexpectedly.

"She's a lovely little girl," I agree, guardedly and wondering what it is he wants from me exactly.

"You're making a great job of bringing her up."

I bite down on the retort that if I am, it's no thanks to him.

Are you planning on being here for long?" I ask, pleasantly.

"Why? Are you trying to get rid of me?" he fires straight back. He's joking, I think but I detect the underlying seriousness in the turn the conversation has taken. I obviously am trying to get rid of him but hurtful as that might be to Jake, it's not fair to Daisy. Honesty causes me to tone down my rhetoric.

"It's just… She's obviously happy you're here. I don't want her hurt by you running out on her again."

He turns back towards me. "Is that what you think I do?" he asks, offended.

"Well, it is, isn't it? Daisy, your job, all the women in your life…"

"I don't mean to run out on Daisy," he protests, vehemently, too vehemently, I feel, from one on whom the responsibilities of parenthood sit so uneasily. "It's difficult."

"I bet."

"I don't want her dragged into the circus that my life has turned into..."

And whose fault is that, I wonder. I plough on like the proverbial steam train. "Daisy's just a little girl and she doesn't understand. I wish you'd be more aware of her, that's all I'm saying…"

He frowns, thinks about what I've said and amazingly, with an imperceptible shrug of his shoulders, seems to accept it. Perhaps it's that causes me to comment on a side of his life basically none of my business. "This woman you profess to love. What does she say about you being here?"

"She's not so happy."

"If you're serious about each other, I'd have thought you'd want to spend time together."

"I'm not sure she feels the same about me…" he answers, carefully.

So that's the problem and now he has shocked me. Mean as it is, I can't help thinking, it jolly well serves him right. The biter bitten at last! But I've forgotten how Jake's always had the ability to sense my every thought and feeling. A closed look settles on his face. Hurt, anger, self-pity, I see it all. He comes back at me again.

"I don't want us to fall out, Bryn. It isn't fair on Daisy…"

That's a neat role reversal if ever there was one and there's nothing I can say, other than, "You're right, of course…"

"We ought to take her out together, show a united front. It would do her good…"

"What here, in Paxos? What about the press?"

"Damn the press! I can't spend my life running away, Bryn…"

"Then don't run away – go home and sort your problems out!"

He shakes his head. "I'd like to spend a few more days here. Then I'll go back and face the music, I promise. And in the meantime, I'm going to make it up to Daisy. A day out together as a family would be a start…"

I can't remember the last time we had such a heart to heart, probably never, come to think of it. And then, what he's just said, penetrates my consciousness, most importantly that he wants to make it up to Daisy. But he has a lot to make up to her, I think. He has a lot to make up to me too, but that's entirely irrelevant.

Daisy has finally become bored of skimming stones and joins us. She finishes off the orange juice Jake's brought and then we return to the villa and to Father, for lunch which, bless him, he has ready and waiting. I have no idea what he thinks of Jake's return because, unusually for him, he keeps his opinion to himself. He greets him civilly enough. Jake's here, he'll make the best of it and in any case, the morning's foray into the village has put him in a better mood than he's been in for a long while. He tolerates Jake for Daisy's sake, as he tolerates Edward for Max and Chloe's. That he thinks me incapable of choosing a mate is clear, a trait he fears, given his choice of my mother, I've inherited. Whilst we eat, Jake chats easily to Daisy. He's on his best behaviour though it won't last forever. Worryingly, there's still no sign of Chloe and Milo, causing me a disquiet I keep to myself, as does Father too, probably feeling, quite rightly, he's meddled enough for one morning. I can't even talk the situation over with Edward as he's gone into Gaius to fetch the hire car and to find Simon, I presume. Hopefully, the walk will aid his recovery. Edward and Simon are the least of my concerns.

Has this holiday really gone so pear-shaped, when we were enjoying ourselves so very much? Or have I only imagined that scenario? After lunch and after we've cleared up, Jake plays board games with Daisy, whilst in the bay below, I see the Christa setting out from port, a toy boat speeding towards the open sea. I've no idea if Milo's on it or even if I want him to be, when it's bound to upset Chloe. Perhaps she's gone for a walk to clear her head and won't want to share her sorrow with me, her mother. I should have talked to her when I'd chance and yet, fearing more argument, I've steered well clear, more shame me. She's seventeen and knows nothing about love but it would have been better by far, if she and Milo had been left to get on with it.

I'm just wondering about a walk into the village to call round at Agatha's for any more news, when that lady herself appears. From the other side of the olives, Boadicea's strident bray betokens her method of arrival. She launches straight in.

"Milo…Milo's clothes are gone…vamoosed…wretched boy…he must 'ave sneaked upstairs and taken when I not looking…"

"You mean he didn't catch the boat?"

"He no catch boat…" she answers, scathingly. "Where's Chloe…where is that damn Chloe…?"

I'm partly bristling at her tone of voice towards my daughter, when it occurs to me that after all, she's only a worried mother, as am I, if the truth be known. "I'm sorry, Agatha, I've no idea where she is. I've not seen her since breakfast. I assumed…hoped…she was seeing Milo off…"

A worrying thought takes root, coiling tendrils of fear around a heart already bruised and shaken. If Milo's taken his clothes and scarpered, then surely, Chloe wouldn't be as crazy as to have gone with him – would she? I look across at Father and see his face, suffused with guilt. Surely, she couldn't have been back to the villa, in my absence and Father simply hasn't told me? Even though he promised that he would!

I spin round and leaving a bemused Agatha behind, I fly upstairs to check her room, the chill fingers of dread crawling the length of my spine at the sight awaiting me there. Why did it never enter my head! Chloe is altogether too strong minded and stubborn – and I can't think who she's inherited it from!

Her room is empty. Her clothes are gone. Given the evidence before my eyes, I have no other alternative than to return downstairs to tell Agatha. Chloe and her precious son, Milo, have run away together and neither of us has the slightest idea where they've gone.

# Chapter Ten

A stream of invective hits me, impossible to follow with only my text-book Greek. I know enough to get the general gist. There's little to be done. The police will keep a look-out for the runaways but they have better things to do, like chasing criminals and tourists! Police are the same the world over it appears. With a haughty stare reserved especially for Edward, the policeman returns his notebook to his top pocket. Agatha sinks into a chair, buries her face in her apron and begins a high-pitched keening wail.

    It's the nice policeman, the football fan, the one who let Edward off the hook and whose first name I've since learned is Errol. Given the average Greek Mamas' penchant for naming their sons after saints, that's a misnomer if ever there was one. It suits him.

    After his attempted reconciliation with Simon, Edward spent yesterday combing the island for the runaways and Jake is out again this morning with Max, who only found out about his sister's disappearance on his late return last night. I wonder if he knows more than he's letting on but he swears not. Father, ably assisted by Daisy, has taken over the running of Agatha's shop, enabling Agatha to pay full attention to her grief, which she does with increasing relish. Milo isn't ever coming back. His life is ruined. All his mama's wonderful plans for his future have turned to ashes and all because of that Jezebel, that Chloe, whom she knew was trouble from the very first moment she clapped eyes on her.

She must take after her mother, Chloe, I mean, not Agatha who has repeated her woes so often, I know them by heart and am hanging onto my temper only with difficulty. I can't believe she's called the police in. Milo's eighteen, for heaven's sake and Chloe nearly so. They have a perfect right to do exactly as they please, even if it doesn't please their nearest and dearest, which it most certainly doesn't, not even me, the senior Jezebel, who has thwarted plans for her offspring too, and all involving further education. I know exactly what I'm going to say when I catch up with her, as I surely must and it's a wonder her ears aren't burning already.

I've yet to recover from Mikey. Oblivious that his youth is against him and he's wasting his time, Errol bats his eyelids at me.

"Is daughter, yes?"

"Yes, I'm afraid she is…"

"You not old enough for daughter nearly grown up."

"Oh, yes. I'm afraid I am…"

"We keep look out. There no more we can do. They no broken law…"

I could have told him this already. Edward leaps up, the distraught father who's had enough and he's playing the role to a tee.

"Are you meaning to tell me, you haven't got every available man out, combing this blasted island? She's seventeen, for heaven's sake – she and this Milo chap can't just have disappeared."

Even when he's sober, Edward, it appears, has a knack of rubbing policemen up the wrong way. Agatha's wails increase in volume, then in case we aren't impressed enough, she emerges from behind her apron and lets rip with a string of excitable Greek I suspect it's a good job we can't understand. She's been busy in the kitchen this morning, assuaging her woes in baking sugared almond cookies and pineapple bread and the room is sweetly scented with her efforts.

Through the doorway, into the shop, I can hear Daisy's excited prattle and Father, holding forth to one of his many customers, who have been arriving in a steady stream all morning, drawn by the excitement which has spread through the village like wildfire. Even now, tender-hearted bosoms are heaving with emotion. The young ones have eloped, run away to be together and no one has the slightest idea where they've got to. There's never been anything so romantic for many a year.

Greeks love a good scandal. Errol draws himself up to his full height.

"This man your husband?" he demands, imperiously.

"We're divorced. Chloe is our daughter though."

"He ought keep better eye on her…"

"Now look here, my man…"

"Edward, losing your temper isn't going to help…" I warn.

I might as well save my breath. Edward lets fly with something unrepeatable for which he's lucky Errol doesn't fling him straight into prison. He's had enough, of all of us, it appears, even me, and with a snort of disapproval, he stalks away. The shop door slams behind him and I doubt we'll see him again, or any other of the island's police force either, little as it is. For all I know, Errol might be the island's police force.

For the moment, there are more important matters to consider, like Agatha's bout of hysterics for one. The best I can do, I sum up quickly, is to remove Edward from the scene before he causes any more trouble. First looking in on Father and Daisy, then assuring Agatha we're only returning to the villa to check Chloe and Milo haven't returned and we'll be straight back if there's news, I hustle Edward out. On the way back, I treat him to a well-deserved piece of my mind.

"You're not helping, anything but in fact…" I finish up, flushing hotly and wiping my brow. It's hot. I'm hot, close to boiling point, in fact.

Edward runs a distracted hand through the remains of his hair.

"I'm out of my mind with worry, Bryn…"

"And you think I'm not?"

"Of course you are…"

"You know what Chloe's like. She's always been impulsive, even as a little girl. Look at when you walked out on us and she sneaked out of school and caught the bus into Derby to find you. She was only eight…" Chloe's childhood and growing up years are littered with her passions and spontaneities, the injured animals she's brought home, the unlikely hobbies and unsuitable friends she's made, the making up her mind about any given issue and refusing to budge, no matter what. Edward flushes.

"I felt like the worse dad out…"

He was right to feel like that but now's not the time to labour the point. He's done his best to make it up to us since.

"You know I've always loved the children. I love you too, in my own way. Just not…"

"Edward, I understand, honest I do but this isn't helping. We have to put Chloe first and think where she might have got to. Have you sorted things out with Simon yet?" I finish abruptly, trying a change of tact. He shrugs noncommittally.

"We're talking again if that means anything…"

"Of course, it does…"

"I've no idea where we go from here…"

"You have to give it time…"

We've reached the villa and as we let ourselves through the gates, at once, I feel steadier, like I've reached a place of safety and that somehow, now we're back here, at Cassiopeia, difficult as life presently is, everything will turn out alright in the end. As we climb the steps to the top terrace, a figure extracts itself from a chair and hurries towards us. It's Simon. Edward frowns.

"Oh, it's you," he says, coldly.

"Edward… I've just seen Jake. He says Chloe's gone missing, that she's run off with Milo…"

"That's just about it."

"I've come straight here to see if I can help…"

"What can you do?" Edward retorts but in tones I wonder how Simon can bear to hear.

"I saw them buying tee-shirts and shorts, at a market stall in Gaius…"

"When! When did you see them…?"

"Yesterday, I'm trying to tell you…"

Simon is only trying to help and it's good to know that at least as recently as yesterday, Chloe and Milo were safe. I jump in with a brief resume.

"She thinks she's in love with him. They must be somewhere close – this island's only eight miles' circumference and they can't have got off it, not on the Christa at any rate because I've checked. Why don't you two have a scout round? Take the car. It can't do any harm…" It'll be a chance for you to talk some more, I conclude, though this last I keep to myself.

I can't, won't allow myself to get too wound up over Chloe who'll return when she's good and ready, I'm convinced. This holiday wasn't meant to split my family up, anything but in fact.

"Edward, I'm sorry!" Simon bursts out and understandably, Chloe not the one uppermost in his mind. He's thinking about Edward and this holiday which was meant to bring them closer together but which instead, has only succeeded in blowing them further apart. This has nothing to do with me. I move to go past him but Edward lays a hand on my arm, gripping it so tightly, I wince.

"This isn't the time," he growls, to Simon, not to me.

"We can't leave things as they are…"

"Why? You were happy enough before…"

"I wasn't happy. I had issues. We just hadn't talked…"

The grip on my arm tightens. Suddenly aware of it, with an apologetic smile, Edward releases me.

"Oh, yes, the little matter of wanting children that you've never bothered to mention…"

"Can I remind you, that despite the trouble your children are presently causing you, you do at least have a family…"

"So that means I can't possibly want more?"

"Why should you? Besides…how could we?" Simon finishes quietly, his words hanging in the air, full of pain, like gun-smoke after the bullet is fired. I can't help myself. Even though it's none of my business, I'm aware that some of this is down to me.

"There are ways," I interrupt, softly. "Adoption for one…or surrogacy…"

Simon looks straight at Edward. "That would just depend, wouldn't it…?"

"You mustn't blackmail him…"

"I'm trying to find out how he feels."

"How I feel?" Edward retorts heatedly. "Being a dad is the very best part of my life. I'd never close the door on doing it again. Hell, I might even manage to get it right next time!"

None of us can believe Edward's just said this, not even Edward. Simon's voice fills with longing and if ever I thought he was using wanting children as excuse to end his relationship with Edward, this alone dissolves the thought.

"You do want children?" he demands, breathlessly.

"I'd like the chance to think about it, at least…"

"Oh, Edward…"

"You should have talked to me…"

"Of course I should…"

"I might even grow to like the idea…"
"Oh, God, I wish you would…"

At this point, regretfully and just when the conversation's getting especially interesting, I extract myself and leave them to it. People should talk more but they never do, not until it's too late. But I'm absolved, forgiven and if I've yet to forgive myself, I've forgiven Simon.

Instead of returning inside, I swing away from the villa, into the welcoming depths of the olive and cyprus trees below the lower terrace, following my instincts and heading for the path by Tomas' garden and noting with satisfaction, it's well on the way to recovery. There's no sign of Tomas. I've not seen Tomas for a day or two and I wonder if he's alright. A forest of greenery thrusts through the rich soil and all around is burgeoning and bearing fruit. This is a lush and fertile island, engendering lush and fertile thoughts. From here, I trace the path of Boadicea's escapade, emerging, minutes later, in the meadow housing Pascal Romano's stolen motorcycle where I stand long moments, mesmerized by sight of the restless sea below, crashing and slapping against the rocks. My brows settle in a thin line of concentration and I throw myself down, draping my arms around my knees and staring out seawards, my head full of Chloe and Milo's elopement and then Lillie and Pascal who tried to elope but failed. Unlike the poor, doomed lovers, Chloe and Milo still have their futures before them and it's only that they're too young, too naive, too stupidly in love to realise, love should be saved for when they're older and life doesn't get in the way.

Life always gets in the way and aren't I the very testament.

As if in mockery of my mood on such a glorious day, the sea carouses joyfully, sending frothy crested wavelets skipping up onto the beach, which linger greedily before receding with a hiss, audible even here, so high above it, the sound carried by the breeze cooling my heated face.

A shadow falls. Startled, I look up to find Jake staring down at me. He sits down next to me, invading my space but then I remember he's been out, searching for Chloe and this mollifies my approach.

"No luck?" I demand, eagerly, his expression telling me what I know already. I'm clutching at straws.

"They've apparently vanished into thin air. Edward and Simon have gone to have another search round…" His hand brushes my arm in sympathy. "You mustn't worry, Bryn," he soothes and sounding so much like he means it, for a moment I even forget it's Jake. Jake, the expert at saying what needs to be said but with no substance to his words.

"I'm not worried about her being in danger as such," I assure him. "I like Milo. He's kind and gentle and he obviously cares for Chloe very much but he's allowed it to cloud his judgement. He's older, he should bear more responsibility. It's not fair of Agatha to keep blaming Chloe all the time. How does she think that makes me feel?"

"I don't suppose she means it, Bryony. She's worried about him missing Uni, as you must be with Chloe…"

"It's such a mess, Jake," I wail. "And I've no idea how to go about putting it right!"

Jake's brows furrow in concentration. "What about Milo's friends? Haven't they any idea where he might have got to?"

Sadly, I shake my head. "That was the first avenue Agatha tried. They all swear they have no idea where he is or Chloe either. They could be lying, of course. They might, probably are, lying low in a friend's villa, in which case, we've no chance of finding them. They've not booked tickets on the Christa – not yet, at any rate. Their office has a description and my mobile number. They'll ring me the moment they try.

We'll just have to sit tight, wait for them to come to their senses…"

"That's just about it, Bryn, I'm afraid."

Our conversation has drawn to its natural conclusion. Jake's tried, everyone's tried but we're no further forward. A wave of misery washes over me. "Isn't it about time you went home, back to England?" I demand, unforgivably, abruptly changing tact whilst pretending to myself I'm only saying it for his own good.

"Not yet," he answers, stiffly, offended, his tone telling me I've interfered in a matter none of my business.

"I'm only asking…"

"Thanks for making me feel not wanted."

"I'm sorry, that's not what I meant. I was thinking about Daisy, that was all…"

"But it's good for Daisy that I'm here, isn't it?"

"Yes…I suppose so…"

Oddly and with a dawning realization, I acknowledge to myself how good it's been to have someone with whom to share the responsibility of Daisy. There's something else too, surprising me even more, the seed of an idea that I'll actually miss Jake when he's gone. Parenting is a two-person business and no one knows this better than me, the woman who's brought up three on my own.

"Jake…if you don't mind me saying…You seem different somehow…"

"Do I? How exactly?"

"As if, at last, you might quite be enjoying being a dad…?"

I've been thinking as I speak and his smile at my words tells me I'm right. Perhaps he's grown up at last, I consider, amazed by it. If he has, it's about time, I muse, a conjecture leaving me with the even happier thought, that Daisy will be the one to reap the benefit. Thoughts of Daisy remind me that leaving her alone with Father for any length of time, is unfair. I leap up.

"I'd better fetch Daisy from Agatha's. I don't want Father overtiring himself."

Jake jumps up, too. "I'll come with you, if you like…"

"That's really not necessary…"

"Please, I'd like to…"

"I'll only be ten minutes."

Aware of his quick frown of annoyance, I swing on my heels and hurry off village-wards, leaving him staring disconsolately after me. Due to his own, inexplicable actions, he's at a loose end, a situation amply explaining his willingness to join in the search for Chloe. It's obvious he doesn't want to resume his football career and I wonder again, beautiful as Paxos is, what trouble he's in at home that's caused him to hide himself away here.

I should have asked him whilst I'd chance.

My steps hasten towards Agatha's shop, where first I have the task of calming its owner, before, with difficulty, extracting Daisy, who naturally doesn't want to leave such a scene of excitement and has no hesitation in telling me so. Father meanwhile, refuses to desert his post, reasoning inarguably, that he can do better here, as stand-in shop-keeper, a profession to which, given the crowd I have to fight my way through even to get into the shop, he appears to have taken to with relish. All I can do is elicit a promise that he won't overdo it. He will, of course. Arguing against the unmoveable force that is my Father is a waste of time and breath.

Buoyed all the way home by Daisy's excited prattle, back at the villa, I find Max. I've not seen my son for a while and he's lounging on the terrace, strumming his guitar. Daisy and Father apart, it's a relief to find someone in this family who is happy and still enjoying their holiday. How uncomplicated he seems.

"Have you seen Jake?" I demand.

"He's come back and gone straight out again. With a face on him like thunder," he warns me, pleasantly. "I think he's gone out to look for Chloe again."

"You might have gone with him, Max…"

"Chloe will come back when she's good and ready, you know she will."

He's right, of course, a voice of reason in a storm of trouble.

"Max, are you sure you don't know where she is?" I ask, suspiciously.

"Honest mum, I've no idea. I'd tell you if I had."

Would he? Do I even know either of my children anymore? Present circumstances suggest that I don't and that it's something I'd better get used to. They're growing up and I can't stop that. I should be combing the island for Chloe but I have Daisy to consider and playing one of the board games we've brought with us, helps to keep both our minds occupied. I'm not sure when I start to worry about Chloe for real but it's after Edward and Simon's return. They've had no luck either.

"Just wait until I find her, I'll give her a piece of my mind," Edward grumbles, still in recovery from his hangover and pouring himself an orange juice which he drinks down in one. Simon has gone straight up to his room. We're on the terrace and Daisy is idling over the Ludo board, listening eagerly to our every word. "She will be alright, Bryn, won't she?" Edward finishes, smiling down at her reassuringly to show her he's not a bit worried though I see from his eyes that he is. The fact he even feels the need to ask, worries me enough. Calm, practical Edward who, belligerent policemen apart, hardly ever gets flustered and who always takes life on the chin, no matter what. Mindful of Daisy, I only shrug my shoulders, telling him through my expression, I'm worried, too.

"If she's not back by tomorrow, I'll pay the police another visit," he whispers, over the top of Daisy's head.

"I'll come with you…"

"Me too!" Daisy squeals, sharp as a tack.

There's no way to keep secrets in this family and there's nothing any of us can do but wait. Wait for Chloe to come to her senses and return home, here to Cassiopeia and put our minds at rest. At least Edward has made it up with Simon but as always, when one problem is solved, it's only for another to rear its head. Odd now to think, I came on this holiday to get away from my problems.

We get through the rest of the day. Father returns from Agatha's with news she's recovered enough to take over in the shop, where he's left her, regaling her customers with tales of the Jezebel, Chloe, who's run off with her precious son. Edward prepares supper and after washing up, I put Daisy to bed. Our party is subdued, even Father and it's by an unspoken consent, we turn in for an early night. Tomorrow is another day, the day when Chloe will be found, I console myself, if not totally believing it. There's no sign of Jake and I can't help thinking that's typical. Bored of looking for Chloe, he's probably holed up in some bar somewhere and hasn't given us another thought.

I'm being unfair. He's done his best and I should give him credit for that.

The island darkens and becomes still, a muffled thickness through which, now and then, the piping squeak of bats penetrates, alongside the mournful hoot of an owl and the odd stirrings and shufflings with which a night is always filled. I can't sleep. As a sliver of silver moon frets at my window, I throw back the sheet, wrap myself in my dressing-gown and pad downstairs to make a mug of tea, taking it out onto the terrace, where I sit, slumped at the table, staring through the darkness and willing Chloe to appear.

"One in the pot for me, dear girl?" a familiar voice enquires. Father. We've been here before.

He can't sleep either. Rubbing vaguely at his chest, he pulls out a chair and sits across from me.

"Are you alright?" I whisper.

"Never felt better, my dear, Chloe apart, of course…" His hand shifts across the table and covers mine. He's worried, too, and I feel a sudden burst of anger that Chloe has so thoughtlessly put us through all this, ruining the holiday, putting Father under strain, when strain is the last thing he needs.

Comforted in our mutual concern, we drink our tea and chat, of this and that, nothing in particular, and then, we return to our respective beds. I want to tell Father that he's doing too much but I don't. I want to wrap him in cotton wool, but he'd hate it if I did. He is as he is and I am as I am and now and then, in the epicentre of the miniature storm this creates, we meet and confer, two people who love and care for each other.

At some point, I fall asleep though I wake with the dawn, the scent of a fresh day filling me with a totally unexpected calm. I rise, get dressed and go downstairs. Chloe's not there, of course, that would be too much to expect. Instead, I discover Jake, sitting hunched over a mug of tea on the terrace. He glances round and crazily, he's smiling.

"You've found Chloe!" I screech, hurrying towards him.

"Don't worry, she's safe."

The use has gone out of my legs. He jumps up and guides me to his chair and all concern, fetches me a mug of tea, which I drink gratefully, waiting for its warmth to activate my senses again.

"Are you sure she's alright?"

"She's absolutely fine…"

"Tell me everything," I demand.

"I'll do better, I'll show you," he returns.

He's not joking. I rush upstairs, shake Edward and Father awake, to give them the news, hardly waiting for their sleepy response before rushing back downstairs to Jake, who has already brought his hire car round to the gates.

With time only for me to hop into the passenger seat we're off, turning out onto the narrow track beyond the villa and on our way. It feels odd to be in a vehicle again and especially one with Jake, jolting and bumping over ruts and pot-holes in a manner excluding conversation, until we turn onto what passes for the main road in these parts. I can't get to Chloe quickly enough.

"Have you talked to her yet?" I demand.

Jake shakes his head. "I made sure she didn't see me. I didn't want to scare her off…"

"When…when did you find her?"

"Last night. I thought it best to fetch you…"

The sense of this information takes a moment to sink in.

"And you've waited all this time?" I snap, scandalized.

"You couldn't have done anything, Bryn, not until it got light at any rate. Besides, I was waylaid, you know how it is. You weren't over-worried, in any case, were you?"

His bald assumption takes my breath away. He probably means he caroused his time away in a bar and must have spent the night where he was and with whoever she was. Jake's irresponsible behaviour is cast in stone and some things never change.

"I was dreadfully worried, actually…" I tell him, frostily

He shoots me a glance. "If I'd told you last night, Edward would have taken over…"

Stolen his moment of glory he means and this is the true reason why he's kept Chloe's whereabouts to himself. He ought to keep quiet before he digs himself in any deeper.

"Chloe is his daughter…" I return, wondering why I have to point this out.

"Perhaps on hindsight, it was wrong but…"

"Honestly, Jake! Where is she?"

"You'll see, shortly…"

I've no idea why he's being so secretive, like a magician, waiting to regale his audience with his final, curtain-dropping trick. We head into Gaius where we park up, walking quickly through the sleepy streets, past the bright flowers tumbling from balconies already hung with washing, and on to the water-front. Shops are opening and the cafes are rolling down their awnings for the start of the day. Everything is right in the world, it appears, other people's worlds, that is and only mine, as usual, a little askew. I follow Jake along the promenade until he brings us to a halt in front of a neat little motor boat bobbing on the quay-side, its name, painted in blue on its side, proclaiming it to be, "The Gypsy Princess'. He undoes the moorings and jumps in, turning to hold out a hand.

"Where are we going?" I burst out, my mind filled with the suspicion that for some crazy reasoning of his own, he's using this as a ploy to get me alone. I didn't use to be so suspicious. He grins and I think, perfectly inconsequentially, that if only his temperament matched his looks, he'd be irresistible.

"You'll see. Do you like her? I've hired her for the week, partly to help with the search for Chloe and partly to show you and Daisy round the island…"

It's never crossed my mind that Chloe could be anywhere other than still on Paxos. The knowledge stuns me into silence. "Tell me where she is, exactly…" I say, quickly.

He gives in at last. "Anti-Paxos. We should have thought of it before…"

Evading his hand, I clamber aboard, searching my mind frantically, meanwhile, for the little I know of the tiny island two kilometres south of Paxos, a scattering of houses apart, almost uninhabited and uninhabitable, the vineyards that support it belonging mostly to families who live on Paxos.

What can she be doing there?

Jake starts the engine and we edge away from the quay-side, steering carefully past the tiny islets of Panayia and Aghios Nikolaos and out into the bay, where I can't resist a last, lingering look back to the mass of silvery green olive trees behind us. Greek Mythology has it that Poseidon created Paxos with his trident, a retreat for lovers and a place to escape to with his mistress. I can believe it, for it's a land of dreams, blurring the edges of reality.

Sea breezes ruffle my hair, dashing spray against my face. I perch on the side of the boat and in an oddly companiable silence, I watch Jake at the wheel, wondering, meanwhile, how and when he's found time to become so skilful with a boat. But then, saving the knowledge he exploded into my life with all the force of an Exocet missile, departing from it just as quickly again, I know so little about him. Nothing good at any rate. A man with the innate ability to turn up in the most unexpected of places. If he really has found Chloe, I'll be eternally grateful to him.

The journey is over quickly, a mere matter of minutes before Anti-Paxos rises into view, at first sighting, a magical green land of olive trees, vineyards and sun-baked rocks if little else. As if he's been at sea all his life, Jake heads us expertly towards a white-gold and silky-sandy beach, framed at either side by what I see, as we draw closer, are two restaurants, each blending into the hillside against which they rest. He manoeuvres us carefully towards a small jetty, cut into the rocks, whereupon he jumps quickly out, reaching over a hand to help me out.

This time, it seems churlish to refuse it.

"Welcome to paradise," he murmurs, jokingly, or at least, I think he's joking.

His hand is warm and firm and closes around mine so naturally that just for a moment, I think…

What I think flies right from my head, for on the terrace of the furthest restaurant, a slim figure appears, a white apron tied over her gaily coloured shorts and tee-shirt. She's lifting down chairs from the table tops, in readiness for the tourists who even now are disembarking from the flotilla of yachts and boats, arriving all around us, as if our presence here has created a tsunami of vessels. The figure looks across and frowns. It's Chloe and I had no business doubting Jake.

Relief overwhelms me. Without another word, I'm off, stumbling up the beach towards her, sand digging into my sandals and dragging at my footsteps but afraid even now that she'll run away before I can reach her and I'll lose her again. I stand before her, struggling to catch my breath, yet still with the sense to acknowledge how well she looks, how lithe and tanned and with her hair tied back highlighting the soft contours of her face. She looks so pretty, so adorable, so wretchedly grown up.

"Oh, it's you," she murmurs and woundingly, her face clouds over.

"Yes, it's me."

"I wondered how long you'd take to find me."

My hopes are instantly dashed.

"Chloe…darling…"

"If you think I'm coming home, Mother, forget it," she says.

## **Chapter Eleven**

A swarthy, middle-aged Greek, in a striped blue and white apron, brings us coffee, the restaurant owner, I suspect, his expression suggesting he knows perfectly well who I am and that if he's agreed to employ Chloe here, he's already having second thoughts about it. I wonder how much she's told him.

Chloe sips her coffee. She's hardly spoken to me yet, a girl no longer but a young woman who knows her own mind. The wind has dropped and beyond the silvery beach stretching endlessly before us, lays an azure blue sea, still and clear as glass. Jake's taken 'The Gypsy Princess' on a tour of the island. I didn't know he could be so tactful.

I return my attention to my daughter. I must remain calm, listen sympathetically to her point of view whilst prompting her to remember I'm her mother and that naturally, I know best.

"What the hell are you doing here?" I hiss, as an opening gambit, not necessarily what I intended.

"I'm working," she answers me, coolly.

"Have you no idea how much upset you've caused? Agatha's out of her mind with worry…"

"She doesn't own Milo."

"Ah, yes, Milo. And where is he exactly?"

"In the kitchens, employed as Assistant Chef."

"Agatha is his mother," I point out, leaving the obvious unsaid, that I'm hers and that Agatha and I both deserve better than the way we've been treated. There's no excuse and in any case, it doesn't appear she's prepared to offer me one. "Your father's upset.

Your grandfather's hardly slept a wink – and at his age, too! You know how ill he's been, Chloe…"

"I'm sorry…"

"You should be…"

"That's emotional blackmail, Mother. I'm surprised at you…"

I'm surprised at myself but this is too important to play fair.

"How dare you place him under this kind of stress?

"I never meant to for an instance…"

"Agatha's reported you both to the police…"

At last I've hit the spot. She bangs her coffee cup down so violently, coffee spills out onto the table. The few customers who've drifted in since we've been here, turn and stare.

"Please, Mother, tell me you're joking…"

"What did you expect?"

"Milo will be furious."

"That's Milo's problem."

"It isn't even as if he's averse to University," she splutters. "He's every intention of resuming his studies once he's finished his gap year."

It's the first I've heard of Milo and a gap year and now it's my turn to be outraged.

"Then why didn't he just say so?"

"He knew what his mother would say. She'd refuse to accept it and that now we're together, everything's changed…"

Her words fall, an earthquake of shattering proportions and there's no way across the chasm it's opened between us. This is serious, more serious than I thought.

"What's changed, Chloe?" I ask quietly, dreading her answer.

She can't wait to tell me. "Milo and I want to be together forever," she retorts, heatedly. "We love each other. There's no way we'll allow anyone to split us up, not even Agatha and certainly not when we've only just found each other…"

All this has been going on under my nose and I didn't even realise. I don't know where to start telling her how crazy this is – as tactfully as possible, of course. "Chloe, don't be such an idiot. I know you imagine that what you feel is for real but it isn't, believe me. It's only playing at love. You're too young for such a commitment. You should be enjoying yourself, living your life to the full. You're not even eighteen yet…"

"I'm perfectly old enough to know my own mind and so is Milo…"

I'm banging my head against the brick wall of her certainty. I inhale deeply and then release the breath slowly. Relaxation technique, good in a crisis and of course it doesn't work. Taking a slug of coffee, I try to find pathways through the chaos of my thoughts.

"You haven't thought this through. If you don't go back to school…"

"Please don't start on that old chestnut again…"

"If you don't go back to school…" I continue, doggedly, ignoring the interruption, "you'll end up in a dead-end job, exactly like this one but it'll be for the rest of your life. You'll be bored silly and worse, wasting your talents! How's Milo going to get through University…?"

"We'll support each other…"

"Don't be ridiculous!"

"We're going to University – together," she points out, patiently, as if, in the interval since last I saw her, there's been some kind of a role reversal and now I'm the child.

"In case you've forgotten, you have no 'A' levels and I'm sorry, my dear girl but there's no way you'll get to University without…" I retort, triumphantly and happily pointing out the one bridge she cannot possibly cross.

Unfortunately, from my point of view, she has it all worked out. "That's just where you're wrong. I'm enrolling at a crammer college in Oxford after the holidays, precisely to finish off my 'A' levels. I've already rung and made preliminary enquiries and they're interested in enrolling me. Milo will find a job. There's plenty of bar work in Oxford, even hotel shifts. I'll work when I can."

"And where are you proposing to live?"

"With a couple of Goth friends going up to Oxford. They're sharing a house and they're looking for someone to help out with the rent. It'll suit us very nicely. When I've passed my 'A' levels and Milo's taught me enough Greek to get by with, I shall enrol at his University in Athens, to study design. You know I've always loved making my own jewellery. I have a talent for it, enough, I think, to make a go of a business, making and selling my own designs. It should blend very nicely with Milo's ambition to run his own photography business…"

She really has thought this through. I open my mouth to tell her this is crazy, that she has no idea what she's talking about when her expression brings me crashing to a halt. She's so young, so touchingly confident and who am I to shatter her dreams, to point out that this scatter-brained scheme is only an illusion, devoid of reality and without a hope in hell of coming to fruition. She'll find that out soon enough and it breaks my heart that she will.

It's crazy…I'm crazy even contemplating giving into her and yet…and yet… She's so determined, so sure she and Milo can surmount every obstacle, whatever life throws at them. Another thought penetrates the fog of my consciousness. She's just admitted, cack-handed kind of way as it is, that I've been right all along. She's determined to sit her 'A' levels, which to me, as a worried mother, is wonderful to hear. Not in the manner I would like and not at school as I'd prefer but she is going to sit them – and having a plan to go to University with Milo off the back of it, is certain to concentrate her efforts.

"God knows what your father will say…" I warn.

Her face lights up. Rightly, she senses I'm weakening, encouraged to it by the undoubtable truth that all my life, I've done my best for her. Spoiled her rotten in other words and now I'm reaping the consequences. I can't bear to see her hurt.

"You mean, you'll back me up?" she demands, breathlessly.

"I mean, we need to talk some more. I must be mad but… Yes, if you can manage to convince me you can make this work, I'll back you up…"

Her whoop of delight turns heads again and this time brings the restaurant owner scuttling out from the bowels of his restaurant, worried we've come to blows I shouldn't wonder. Milo trails after him, his gaze alighting on me nervously before shooting an adoring glance in Chloe's direction which she returns in full measure. I have plenty to say to that young man but now isn't the time.

"I need to take the day off, Mr. Michelakos, if that would be okay?" Chloe demands of her employer, unfazed when his face clouds over.

"Ah…no…no Chloe. This not good idea. You needed here!" he retorts, in passable English.

"Are you going back?" Milo bursts out.

"I need to see Grandpa. I'll be back first thing tomorrow…" she promises.

Milo moves protectively towards her and taking her hand, he strokes it gently. They're so tactile with each other, so in love and to an old romantic like me, it's perfectly delightful.

"I come, too. I have to face my mother some time…" he murmurs.

He's right, of course, though Mr. Michelakos, understandably is even more reluctant to lose two members of staff than he is to lose one. In typical Greek fashion, he throws his hands in the air and begins to argue, hotly and volubly but amazingly, after a deal of soothing and polite noises from Chloe, to which the rest of the restaurant's customers listen in with great interest, it appears he's prepared to give way. All Greeks, it appears, love lovers, Agatha accepted, of course.

"You come back tomorrow or no job waiting…" he warns, in a vain attempt to seize control of a situation fast spinning away from him.

"We'll be back…" As demonstrative as a Greek herself, Chloe throws her arms around his considerable girth and hugs him, a process he appears to enjoy.

It takes only a moment for Milo to fetch their haversacks from inside the restaurant and before Mr. Michelakos can argue the point further and to cheers and general applause from the restaurant's customers, we depart, dropping down onto the beach to circumnavigate the numerous bikini-clad bodies, draped across towels, to the jetty beyond and to where, as if by a divine osmosis, 'The Gypsy Princess' has reappeared.

Jake heaves too, then waits patiently for us to board. I'm reeling from the success of our mission and yet unsure whether I want most to hug the runaways or simply brain them. I'm delighted to have my daughter back and to know that she's safe. Jake says nothing, telling me by the slightest rise of one eyebrow, how amazed he is they've given in so meekly. He expected more trouble and so did I.

The morning is rattling on and I can't wait to get back to Cassiopeia. Without further ado, Jake opens the throttle and we set off, leaving Anti-Paxos quickly behind us and leaving curling waves, frothed with lace, in our wake. In an amazingly short time, we've reached Gaius, where we moor the boat, collect the hire car from the car park and return home, in time for the end of what appears to have been a lingering breakfast. A happy family gathering, enhanced by the splendid news of Chloe's discovery.

The scene before us erupts at our appearance and there ensues a deal of hugging and crying and exclamations of delight. If Chloe didn't realise before how much she's been missed, she must do now. So far so good but it appears the Paxos grapevine has already swung into action. Barely has Edward time to recover his equilibrium and remember his dignity enough to demand of the runaways, what the hell they think they've been up to, worrying us all to death, when a small, plump figure hurtles up the terrace steps towards us. It's Agatha. From beyond the olive trees, Boadicea heehaws her own, unique opinion of events, which doesn't happen to be favourable.

Circumnavigating Father, executing a dance of joy with Daisy around the table, Agatha heads straight for Milo and throws her arms around him, covering him with kisses and tears, meanwhile directing a volley of incomprehensible Greek towards him that obviously embarrasses the poor lad. He doesn't know what to say and neither does anyone else and an awkward situation is fast developing. Seizing her chance, Agatha turns on Chloe and lets fly, all in Greek fortunately so we miss the worst of it.

But then, with a warning sixth sense, I glance towards Father, alarmed to see that he's stopped dancing and is standing rubbing at his chest and breathing heavily. He wipes a hand across his forehead and sits down abruptly. His ruddy colouring has faded. Suddenly, the scene before me goes into slow motion, coalesced into the sight of that rotund, pocket dynamo, my Father, sitting looking vaguely surprised, as if a thought has just occurred to him which he has no idea how to elucidate.

"Are you alright?"

"Of course I am, dear girl. A little indigestion, that's all…"

Warning bells are already ringing.

"How long have you had it?" I ask sharply, trying to remain calm and failing miserably.

"It's just a little niggle, nothing to trouble over. It kept me awake in the night…"

I'm on the phone to the medical centre on the outskirts of Gaius, before anyone has chance to draw breath, Father included, though he protests volubly when he realises what I'm doing. But this scenario is just what I've been dreading and how many times have I warned him! I'm irrationally angry. This is precisely what I've been banging on about and he's refused to listen to.

Everything becomes a blur of anxious faces after this and of no one knowing quite what to say or do, me included. I'm worried and as usual, I bottle it up, leaving me with the sensation of a knot, drawn tightly around my chest, restricting my breathing. Within so short a space of time, a young but brightly efficient doctor arrives and whilst I treat him to a potted version of Father's medical history, he whips out his stethoscope, undoes Father's shirt and listens to his chest. Father sits back and frowns. The doctor frowns back at him. Finally, he straightens up.

"We get him into hospital on Corfu. Just to be on safe side, yes?"

Father's never lived on the safe side yet but I don't say as much. Instead, I squeeze his hand, ridiculously reassured when he squeezes it back.

"The heart will break, but broken live on," he murmurs, pathetically and if only I weren't so concerned, I'd accuse him of milking the situation. Blasted Byron and blasted man, what does he mean by it! Momentarily, I'm blinking back tears but fortunately, only Jake notices. He rubs my shoulder and I glance at him gratefully.

But then, the procedures on the island for dealing with emergencies, swings impressively into action. Seemingly only moments later, an ambulance arrives and two uniformed ambulance men and a nurse jump out, load Father into a chair and cart him off to take him to the port, where I'm informed, the Despina -P, the boat used for the island's emergencies, is ready waiting.

Unasked, I scramble into the back of the ambulance after him, whilst Edward and Simon, Max and Chloe and Daisy, who refuses to be left behind, follow behind in the car. Jake, Milo and Agatha volunteer to stay at the villa, to take care of anything that needs doing but with a promise from me, to Jake, that I'll ring as soon as there's news.

If only for Daisy's sake, we're bright and breezy, all hiding the fact we're worried – how could we be anything else. The drive to the port is an endless nightmare, though I guess the driver does his best with the wretched roads he has to cope with. It's enough to shake the patient to death but once we've arrived at the port, they transport him easily enough aboard the Despina-P where we're quickly joined by the rest of our party, together with the nurse, who is accompanying us to the hospital.

We set off, speeding out of the bay, on what seems the endless voyage from Paxos to Corfu and with nothing to do but kick our heels and wait, meanwhile casting surreptitious glances in Father's direction and hoping and praying that his condition doesn't deteriorate. He's complaining but does that mean his condition is worse or should we take some comfort from it? He's cross at all the fuss but that's just Father and he'll have to put up with it.

I accompany him aboard the ambulance, ready waiting for us at Corfu port as the Despina - P docks and which, blue lights flashing, transports us to a surprisingly modern hospital, situated in the centre of town. Edward organizes a taxi and assures me the rest of the family will follow on as quickly as possible. Life has become surreal, with an edge, sharp as an axe. It's so unfair, just when, collectively speaking, this family is on the up again.

Inside the hospital, a phalanx of nurses and doctors descend upon us and Father is rushed away through swing doors, into the heart of the hospital. A sympathetic nurse directs me to a bench in a sterile corridor, through which white-coated figures flit like ghosts. Minutes later, Edward's face swings into view and I'm surrounded by family again. There's comfort in numbers and comfort in this family, dysfunctional or not.

"How is he?" he demands, anxiously.

At that moment, from afar, we hear Father roar. "Your guess is as good as mine," I complain, springing up. "They told me to wait here and that's all I know…"

We do wait, for what seems like forever but is probably only a couple of hours, which we fill by drinking copious cups of excretable coffee and imagining the worst. Doctors the world over, leaving relatives kicking their heels whilst they get on with whatever it is doctors get on with.

All at once, as if in response to our collective anguish, the swing doors fly back and a white-coated figure appears, a benign, stocky figure with grizzled grey hair, his heavily-lined face washed with tiredness, as if he has more on his plate than with which he can reasonably cope. We rush and surround him, all talking at once, even Daisy, who stands, tugging at his coat and demanding that he make her Grandpa better again. He pushes thick, horn-rimmed glasses firmly along his nose and smiles down at her before holding up one imperious hand. We quieten instantly.

"How is he?" I burst out into the silence, dreading what I'm about to hear.

Unexpectedly, his mouth twitches. "As well as can be expected…" he says but with something amazingly like a twinkle in his eye. His head nods rapidly. "For such a bad case of indigestion, he doing remarkably well…"

His words take a moment to sink in.

"But it's his heart, doctor," Edward observes, uncertainly.

"Ah, not his heart…"
"Are you sure?"
"You tell me, I don't know job…?"

"Of course not but…"

"His heart okay. Maybe a little…how you say…frayed round the edges from trouble he had before…months ago, he tell me… But now he strong, healthy man and well as possible…" There's a definite twitch to his lips now. He pats Daisy's head. "No…indeed no…No heart attack but in-di-gestion… Too much cake, he tell me. Give him bad pain…" he murmurs, articulating the words carefully as if we are idiot children which is exactly how we feel after making all this fuss. Agatha's sugared almond cookies and pineapple bread, spring to mind and Father, helping out in the shop, too temptingly on hand to eat more than was good for him! So much for the health-giving benefits of the Mediterranean diet. He always did have a sweet tooth, compounded by a total lack of will power.

After all the upset, the relief at this news is too much to take. I thought he was dying, that his heart was on the point of giving out and all along, he's nothing but a petulant old fraud! Chloe bursts into tears and I put my arms around her.

"Oh, thank goodness. Thank you, doctor, thank you," I babble, over the top of her head.

"You take him home, yes?"

"Aren't you even going to keep him in?"

"No, take him home, please, we wash our hands of him…" The doctor's shoulder's lift. They've checked the patient over and run their tests and he's a disappointment, unworthy of their efforts. They would like to be rid of him. Greek medical services are much like ours, it appears and an empty bed is a freed-up space, like gold-dust.

Edward is already punching numbers into his mobile. Through the swing doors, looking slightly battered, Father appears. Unsure of his bearings and upset by his unexpected tangle with the Greek medical services, he's looking round for someone to blame. Me, of course. His eyes flash with ill-temper. It's my fault. I'm the one who panicked and called the emergency services. Relief washes over me.

"I told you there was nothing wrong," he grumbles, peevishly.

"How's your indigestion…?"

"Gone…unbelievably… The ticker's okay…"

"I know, the doctor said…"

"A storm in a tea-cup…"

"Thank goodness."

And that, it appears, is that, the total of our discussion on the state of his health. If it's shaken him up he won't admit it. I want to throw my arms around him but I don't. I want to tell him he's scared me to death but I don't do this either. We'll never change and it's no good pretending otherwise. Occasionally we reach out and find each other. More often than not, it's only to discover our respective portcullis' clanged shut, cutting us off from our very best intentions.

Uninhibited as ever, Daisy throws her arms around him. Chastened, fuelled by guilt and relief, in equal measures, Chloe puts her arm through his and lays her head upon his shoulder.

"We'd better get a move on," Edward observes briskly. "We've a taxi booked from the hospital to the port. We don't want to miss the ferry and be stuck on Corfu until tomorrow morning…"

No one wants to hang around. It's good to shake the antiseptic smell of the hospital from our heels and emerge into good fresh air, for a short wait before the taxi-bus pulls up in front of us, a requisite for our numerous and noisy party. Cheerfully, we pile aboard and set off, swinging out into the road, careering gaily past dusty, higgledy-piggledy streets of cluttered shops and cream and yellow, sun-baked buildings, a short journey before we're disgorged onto the port, to the welcome sight of The Christa.

Edward hurries off to the ticket office to collect our tickets. Dishevelled and tired from their respective flights, a straggly line of tourists are already waiting to board, their cases and bags tossed from one crew member to another, into the depths of the hold. At that moment, I remember Jake and pulling my mobile from my pocket, I ring him hastily. I guess he can tell by my voice that everything is fine. It feels good to hear his voice, even better to give him the news.

"All's well that ends well, then…?"

"We're on our way back, Father included. We're just waiting to board The Christa…"

His voice sounds as close as if he's standing right next to me. "You're not going to believe this but I'm just coming into the port. You'll see me if you look out into the bay. I was fed-up kicking my heels waiting for news, I was on my way to find you," he continues, sounding disappointed. "Milo's keeping an eye on the villa. Agatha's gone home, thank God."

Suddenly, I see him, a lone figure at the wheel of 'The Gypsy Princess'. I wave and he waves back.

"Oh…goodness… I'm sorry, Jake…"

"Just as long as you're all alright. I'll turn back. I'll probably beat you back into Paxos…"

He really has surprised me this time but that's Jake. My mind is working furiously at this news and my gaze alights on Father, sharing a joke with a crew member from the Christa, as if he's just come from a Chambers meeting rather than the hospital and a matter of life and death. It's not as if there's anything wrong with him and in any case, Edward and Simon will make sure he doesn't over exert himself. 'The Gypsy Princess' curves away in an arc, leaving an expanse of white foam in her wake. I'm impulsive to a fault.

"No…don't go yet, Jake!" I burst out. "Turn back and I'll come and find you. There's something I need to do here, in Corfu, if you wouldn't mind waiting and taking me back with you later…"

It's a big ask and yet he asks no questions. With a little stab of joy, I see 'The Gypsy Princess' swing round in a full circle. In the meantime, ignoring Edward's penny-pinching grumbles about the wasted ticket he's just purchased and with as little explanation as needs be as to why I'm not returning to Cassiopeia with the rest of the party, I manage to extricate myself. My business here is nothing to do with anyone else. Ferries to Paxos are few and far between and Jake's arrival is fortuitous, prompting me to an action, more a half-baked idea than a reality, that has been bubbling away at the back of my mind since I got here.

I march over to Father.

"Other than sitting with your feet up, you're to do absolutely nothing when you get home to Cassiopeia," I warn.

"Oh, I wouldn't dare!" he exclaims, testily. Father hates being told what to do.

"Don't worry, I'll make sure he behaves," Chloe chips in.

"You'll keep an eye on Daisy, too, until I get back? I promise I won't be long."

"Of course, we will, won't we Max?"

My son's nod of agreement is enough. I tear myself away and hurry back along the quayside. Between a clapped-out, rust-coloured fishing-boat, partly submerged underwater and an elderly yacht that's long seen better days, I find Jake, fastening the moorings of his boat, his tall, broad-shouldered figure already capturing the interest of a couple of Greek girls, who happen to be passing. He straightens up and flashes the prettiest girl, one of his famous smiles. But then he sees me and his smile fades. Looking slightly embarrassed, he flaps one hand towards me.

"I'm glad your Father's okay…" he murmurs, when I reach him. Jake and Father have history and I'm surprised how sincere he sounds. He means it and that is surprising.

"Mmm, me too. Are you sure you don't mind about this?"

"What's it about, Bryn?"

"Someone I need to look up. Trouble is, other than they live in the old part of town, I'm not sure where it is exactly…" I stop and blush. I'm acutely aware why I've struggled to confide any of this to anyone. They'd think I was crazy, that I'm chasing after a dream, my only desire being a need to satisfy an insatiable curiosity on a matter none of my business. But I can't help it if Lillie Drachmann's story has got to me and I'm desperate to find out more.

I take a deep breath and launch in.

"I'm looking for a Greek woman called Eleni Mitsopoulos, who used to be the housekeeper at Cassiopeia around Lillie Drachmann's time. You remember I told you about Lillie, the young girl who married Stefan, the previous owner of Cassiopeia, just before the outbreak of the Second World War? Eleni must be a very old woman by now but Agatha says she's moved in with her daughter, who lives in Corfu Town. I've so little to go on but I thought I could ask around…"

Amusement dances in Jake's eyes. He's burning to ask me more but, unusually reticent, he restrains himself. "Sure," is all he says.

We cross a car park and taking our lives in our hands, dodge oncoming traffic, to cross the busy main road running alongside the port, then point ourselves in the direction of the town, only a short walk away. A tumble of ancient, pastel-shaded dwelling houses and shops between Venetian style fortresses, erected on the broad part of a peninsula. After the peace and quiet of Paxos, it's a riot of colour and noise and it takes some getting used to, leaving me wondering what I'm doing here with Jake of all people. He's bound to think I'm mad if I tell him what this is about. That there's something about Cassiopeia. That for reasons not yet clear to me, the place has got under my skin, exuding some dreamy, magical quantity that leaves me convinced we're meant to be here.

It doesn't matter what Jake thinks – why should it matter what Jake thinks! All the same, I'm glad of his company. Past a sun-baked Square, home to a pink and white Orthodox Cathedral gazing upon us benignly - two foreigners, lost and disorientated in an increasingly exotic land - we plunge through an archway, into a labyrinth of narrow streets, paved with cobblestones. It's the old part of town and for a moment, the cacophony of noise nearly deafens us. People hurrying here, there and everywhere, all appearing to know exactly where they're going and jabbering in a language we can't understand. Impulsively, I stop an ancient, bent-backed, old crone, dressed from head to toe in black who hobbles out in front of us from a darkened doorway.

"Do you know of a woman called Eleni Mitsopoulos?" I ask her, in carefully pronounced English. Frustratingly, though I sense she understands me perfectly, she shakes her head. We're strangers and have no business here, the same response I meet from everyone I stop and ask, young and old alike, amongst them, a smattering of tourists who, eager enough as they are to help, haven't a clue what I'm talking about.

I'm hot and bothered and longing to get out of the relentless heat beating down upon our unprotected heads. No one, it appears, knows of Eleni Mitsopoulos and even I'm beginning to wonder if she's merely a product of my over-active imagination. And then, from the dappled doorway of a church, with walls of the softest rose petal pink, a priest emerges, an elderly man with a straggly, pepper and salt beard, his face carved with a network of wrinkles but through which shines the clearest blue eyes I've ever seen.

"Yes, my child?" he asks, in perfect English.

"I was wondering, Father, do you know of a woman called Eleni Mitsopoulos?"

"Eleni? Yes, I know Eleni…" He nods and folds his hands together, his gaze alight with a curiosity he's too polite to satisfy. Instead, he directs me to the bottom of the street, past a walled garden spilling bright-red geraniums and upon which sits an emaciated, flea-bitten and one-eyed cat, cleaning its whiskers, to a narrow street beyond and midway down it, to a tiny shop crammed with trays of exotically coloured fruit and vegetables and jars of olives and bottles of oil, crammed on the shelves. This, it appears, in rooms above it, is where Eleni Mitsopoulos lives. Sensing my rising excitement, Jake follows me, watching me curiously as, overcome with unexpected nerves, I hover at the shop entrance, trying to gather my confidence enough to venture inside.

# Chapter Twelve

We're a giddy six floors up, relaxing at a table on the roof-top restaurant of the Hotel Athena, with its stunning views over the old town and further out, to the sight of the afternoon's sun dipping over deep blue water dotted with gaily coloured boats. I'm grateful Jake's asked me no questions concerning all I've discovered from Eleni Mitsopoulos about Lillie Drachmann and her life, concentrating instead on negotiating us through the busy streets, to this tourist hot-spot, where the staff nearly fall over themselves showing us to the best table. I'd forgotten what it's like being out with Jake, the way his fame goes before him, even here, so many miles from home.

I haven't eaten all day; food has never crossed my mind. I've been too busy persuading Chloe back home and then dealing with Father's non-existent heart attack, which after frightening us all to death has turned out to be nothing more than indigestion. If this was a book, you couldn't write it and I can't help thinking, even on holiday, sometimes life just gets too much.

That the day could have ended in tragedy doesn't need saying.

Jake sits, arms folded, watching through narrowed eyes, my ineffectual attempts with the Baklava he's ordered – filo pastry stuffed with nuts and dipped in honey. I can't eat it.

"At least try!" he orders. Startled into action by his uncompromising stare, I do exactly that. He pushes my coffee cup towards me and I drink this too, grateful this shuts him up.

"Did you find out what you wanted to know?"

"Mmmm…but it's difficult to put into perspective yet…" I murmur.

After spending over an hour in Eleni's company, a diminutive figure, dressed in black, more like a doll than a living, breathing human being, I've yet to absorb the incredible story she's told me. Any misgivings I'd suffered that she might not want to talk to me, a stranger, vanished the instant she fixed me with a keen gaze flecked with a surprising humour. An old woman, crippled with arthritis, sitting alone in a room crammed with family mementoes and photographs on every available surface. She wanted to talk; to re-live her youth and it never occurred to her why I should want to know of her relationship with Lillie Drachmann and the Villa Cassiopeia.

"This Eleni, she worked at Cassiopeia?" Jake probes.

"Until just after the war," I agree, "and then she went to work in a hotel in Athens, where she met her future husband. She only came here, to live with her daughter a few years ago, after her husband died…"

"And she's kept in touch with Lillie Drachmann?"

"Not at first. They lost contact during the war and for many years after it she had no idea what had happened to her after she'd been smuggled out of Paxos. She could have died for all Eleni knew. It happened all the time in those days, people just vanished. She made efforts to find her, of course, even to the point of tracing the German branch of the Drachmann family, only to discover, poor souls, every single one had died in a German Concentration camp."

"But she did find her eventually?"

"It was fate, she said. She was finished working at the hotel when her children were born but her husband still worked there. It was years afterwards when there was some event for the hotel workers and their families. Naturally, Eleni went, too, but with no idea that Lillie was a guest there, at the hotel. One of the children was ill, and she was taking her back home and took the lift to the ground floor. When the doors opened, Lillie was just there…"

I'm plunged again into that little room, with its stifling warmth and its windows and balcony door flung wide onto the tiny enclosed space overlooking the old town and crammed with terracotta pots, planted with dusty-red geraniums. The room crackles with tension and as Eleni Mitsopoulos recounts to me her joy in seeing Lillie again, her rheumy old eyes are bright with tears.

She leans forward in her chair, her bony, age-spotted hands knotted together so tightly, the veins stand out. She speaks in remarkably good English, a distinct voice, deep and rich for such a tiny figure and undiminished by age.

"So out of the blue, so unexpected, as the lift doors open, there I see my dear Lillie, as if a magician has conjured her up out of my head – we knew each other at once but other than to cry and exclaim and fold each other into our arms, neither of us know what to do or to say. Everyone look. All the hotel guests, the bartenders and maids, even the lift-boy. What is this spectacle, they say but we didn't care…"

"But where had she been all those years?" I chip in, eagerly.

Eleni's memory of that time is vivid still. Her thin shoulders lift, her whole body filled with life, as she tells me why, for years, Lillie Drachmann disappeared from the face of the earth. "You must remember, the man she loved, the man with whom she planned to spend the rest of her life, died so tragically. Poor Pascal! His young bones resting at the bottom of the Ionian Sea. She wanted for no-one ever to find her again, as if she never existed…"

"And what of Stefan, her husband…?"

"Ah, Stefan, he very good man. When he found out about Lillie and Pascal, he tried to understand, I think, that Lillie was young and couldn't help herself, that he was old man and shouldn't have married her – and that she shouldn't have married him! No one could undo what was done. Poor Stefan, undeserving of his end…"

"Is that why she didn't go back to Cassiopeia? Because of what happened to Stefan?"

Eleni shakes her head. "At first, after the war, with her little money, she make her way to Germany. Here, she hope to pick up the threads of her life again, only to find, when she get there, her family, all gone and news she knew in her heart already, Stefan gone, too, put to death in camp, the moment he arrived. A whole family wiped out – as if they had never been!" Eleni's frame quivers and her hands lift, palm upwards, a gesture of mute appeal but also a negation of those terrible times. "But no, my Lillie, she not

return to Cassiopeia. The situation, the guilt she felt…
You understand. Better she thought, to disappear than
return to place with too many memories and where
people blame her for her husband's death…"

"But it wasn't her fault…"

"Some would disagree…" Eleni returns,
matter-of-factly, an old woman who understands
human nature and to what extremes the passions can
lead. I lean forward, listening avidly. "But now she
live with the consequences of all that has happened.
She left alone, a young girl, broken by fate and
without returning to Cassiopeia, without ability to
claim, as Stefan's wife, all that is rightfully hers…"

"What did she do?"

"She remembers that before he married her,
and before expedience sent him home, to Paxos, to sit
out the war, Stefan spent his days travelling, a rich
man, indulging his whims by seeing all there is to see,
whatever and wherever took his fancy. A man who
made few friends but one, whom Lillie remembered
and of whom Stefan often talked with great affection.
A man who was the family lawyer and shared his
client's passion for art, an Italian by birth, by name of
Filippino Grippe. As good fortune have it, Lillie met
him once, on the day she and Stefan wed. The
ceremony was only days before war broke out, when,
in token of his friendship with Stefan, Filippino travel
to Paxos, to be best man. All she remember was his
kindness to her and that he lived in Sorrento."

"So she went there to find him?" I demand,
my mind leaping ahead.

"She went to Sorrento and asked around and,
in the natural course of events, an old woman directed

her to his villa in town. He recognised her and, if only for his old friend's sake, he took her in, the one man who know her to be rightful owner of Stefan's wealth..."

As I recount most, if not all, of everything I've learned today, I see I've caught Jake's interest. But in the process of telling him, before I reach the most important part and the bit that I've not got my head round yet, I run out of steam. The heat, the day, the feeling that all I've learned from Eleni shouldn't be subject for common gossip, not even with Jake. I grind to a halt and wipe a weary hand through my hair.

"Do you mind if we stop? I will tell you the rest only, just not for a bit. I need to think..."

"You must be tired. It's been some day," he murmurs sympathetically. He finishes his coffee, then looks at me uncertainly, unusually for Jake, normally so sure of everything and most of all himself.

"Bryony... There's something I've been meaning to say...ask...that is..."

"Ask away. Please!" I smile, pleasantly.

"Something I've been thinking awhile..."

"Tell me, please..."

"I'm not sure where to begin..."

"Jake! For heaven's sake, whatever it is, spit it out!" I don't mean to sound so sharp and the fact that I do, I put down to tiredness. The day's been too much, enough for anyone. Jake's petulant frown reminds me how much he likes to get his own way.

"It'll save for later," he says, huffily.

"Oh but..."

"We ought to get back…"

Home to Cassiopeia and I can't think of any place I'd rather be. He signals the waiter, settles the bill and we leave, descending to ground floor in the lift and then hurrying quickly back through the dwindling streets towards the port.

Back aboard 'The Gypsy Princess', other than the necessities that need saying, we don't talk much, both too self-absorbed, I expect, me with all I've learned from Eleni Mitsopoulos and trying, if failing, to put it into perspective, Jake just subdued and not himself though I've no idea what his problem is. He's probably just fed-up. The day's been a drain on us all. As we speed away, out of the harbour, the sun is dropping low in the sky, trailing a golden path over the sea, as if the waves are parting, just for us and pointing the way home to Cassiopeia. Back in Gaius, we tie up the boat and head quickly back along the promenade. I've hardly given Father a thought since I saw him back onto 'The Christa' and I feel guilty about this now.

The faint strains of guitar music, drifting through the gathering gloom, draws us on and as we approach the waterfront café where Alex works, I realise it's Max who's playing and that he must have gone home to fetch his guitar and returned here, to Gaius. For so early in the evening, the place is unusually thronging, mostly young folk and mostly grouped around my son, I discover when I stop and peer inside. He's sitting on a high stool by the bar, part of the crowd and yet aloof from it, so absorbed in the world he's created through his music, it blots out all else. Even now, accepting of his talent as I am, I can't believe it's Max, nor who or where he gets it from.

Puffed up with pride, wanting to stop and listen some more, instead, I tear myself away and walk on, if acutely aware of Jake's wry grin of amusement. If he says anything, I'll kill him. Any parent has a right to be proud of their child. We locate the car and he drives us home, our discourse reduced to an oddly companiable silence, until, a few short minutes later, we're pulling up outside the gates of Cassiopeia. Unexpectedly, I think of the day we first arrived, a disparate, restless crowd whose only certainty was that we'd made a mistake in coming here.

Edward's already busy with supper. Simon and Daisy are playing board games at the kitchen table. Chloe and Milo are nowhere in sight and Father is for once doing what he's told and is lying stretched out on the recliner on the terrace, a glass of wine by his side. Daisy leaps up and throws herself at Jake and Simon willingly vacates his place, so she and Jake can spend some time together. Heaven knows, she's had little enough attention from her parents of late. After I've assured myself of Father's well-being, I take the opportunity to corner Edward and in case Chloe hasn't already, I tell him of her plans.

"She can't be serious, Bryony…?"

"She is and at least this way, she's determined on 'A' levels and university…"

"But she hardly knows the boy…"

"She's in love with the boy and in any case… We'll be around to pick up the pieces if and when it goes wrong," I tell him resolutely, meanwhile, trying to convince myself our daughter's not gone completely crazy.

Sensing he needs time to consider this unexpected development, I disappear outside, onto the terrace, my gaze drawn to the level of Father's wine glass. There's only a glass or so gone from the bottle but is that the only bottle opened today? I'm too tired to check the wine cellar.

"Just the one, my love," he assures me, raising his glass. "After the day I've had, you surely don't begrudge me?"

Is that a question, or a statement of fact? I'm too tired to doubt and desperate to believe, even Father, even after a lifetime of half-truths and evasions.

"Make sure it is just the one. Where are Chloe and Milo?"

"Gone to Agatha's to sort things out, Lord help them…"

I peer at him closely. He looks happy enough, if a tad tired, hardly surprisingly.

"Are you sure you're alright?"

"Fools are my theme, let satire be my song…" he returns pleasantly, illogically and sounding remarkably like he's in his cups. In other words, on top form and as if today's shenanigans are a mere figment of my overheated imagination. Someone sticks a glass of wine in my hand, Edward, I think and I plonk myself, exhausted, into a chair. Father's reading Byron and now and then regales me with a line.

"Of what is the spirit made? What is worth living for and what is worth dying for? The answer to each is the same. Only love…" he intones, solemnly. "Wouldn't you agree, my precious?"

He's missed his vocation. He should have been on the stage. But then I properly consider the worth of the lines he's just quoted and I pray they're not true because if they are, it means I've made one huge mess of my life. A thought sitting uneasily with my present mood which, aided by another slug of wine and then a top up, thoughtfully provided by Simon, is becoming pleasantly blurred. Suddenly, my glass is empty and on an empty stomach and exhausted as I am, it's too much. I'm grown up, I should have had more sense but sometimes, I am my father's daughter and suffer an impulse to drink myself into oblivion.

Sensibly, I decide on a walk to clear my head and leaving the terrace via the steps, make my way, a little haphazardly, along the track which springs like a broken artery, away from the villa. Avoiding the squabbling hens, stepping over stones and avoiding pot-holes, hardening my heart against the emaciated cats, too numerous to count, I walk on until I come to the gate in the wall, leading into the meadow and this time of the evening, full of the heady scent of wild flowers.

It's intoxicating and beguiling and I pause, basking in its sweetness, my heart swelling with some soft, strange emotion of which I'm only just aware. Below me, obscured by bushes, is the corrugated shed, housing Pascal Romano's stolen motor-bike. I don't know why I've come here, as if I'm drawn, as if I'm unable to leave the happenings at Cassiopeia alone, worrying at it like a cat after a mouse. The remains of the day's light lingers, pouring down from golden heavens and trailing tender fingers over the tranquil sea, an evening for lovers, I think, inconsequentially, throwing myself down on the grass and at last with time enough to consider everything Eleni has told me of the scatterings of Lillie Drachmann's life. Did she and Pascal sit here, I wonder, discussing their future together? They had no future and it was a kindness they didn't know it. No wonder, after Pascal died, so tragically, Lillie faded away, like a ghost, reduced to living her life travelling restlessly around Europe, following the footsteps of her husband, perhaps in repentance of the harm she and Pascal had done.

"Penny for them?" asks a voice, jolting me from my reverie.

It's Jake. He sits down carefully beside me and I think, we've been here before and not so many days ago. "She died, Jake!" I blurt out, emptying my head of its dominating thought and telling him now, so abruptly, what I couldn't bring myself to tell him before.

He's no idea what I'm talking about. "Who died?"

"Lillie and unbelievably, it was only a few days ago. I missed her by a whisker and if I'd only gone last week, I would have met her in the flesh…"

Even now, I can't get my head around this fact, nor how cruel is fate.

"I'm sorry, Bryony…"

"The doctors told her she was dying. Eleni and her daughter took her in and cared for her but even then, other than the priest, she wouldn't let Eleni tell her friends and acquaintances she was there. Eleni and her daughter passed her off as an old friend…"

"She was the owner of Cassiopeia after all?"

I'm fired up, eager to tell him everything now – or nearly everything. "That's just it. She wasn't. Many years ago, she made Cassiopeia over to someone else, some who knew all about her and her life. I'm not sure it's my right to tell you who it was…"

Surprisingly, he accepts my reticence without demur.

"Has it been worth the trouble finding out? Did you really need to know?"

"It has but I can't explain it. I needed to know because…I just needed to know…" I finish lamely, pathetically but I can make no more sense of it than that. Afraid Jake's going to quiz me further, I move the conversation quickly on.

"I've never thanked you properly for putting up with me today."

"Don't be silly…"

"I mean it. You didn't have to do all that. You really have changed," I tell him, realising, as soon as the words are out of my mouth, I've been thinking this awhile.

"You mean I've stopped thinking about myself so much?" he comments dryly, not even a question but an acceptance of fact. I wonder if I've offended him. "It's true what you said before, Bryony. I realise how lucky I am to have Daisy in my life. That she's the important one, after all," he mutters, but then, as if he's no idea how to proceed, he grinds to a halt. Staring resolutely out to sea, he frowns. "I got to thinking something else, too. That…that I was…stupid to throw away what we had before. What happened between us, I mean us splitting up, it was all my fault."

That's some statement and hearing it from Jake's own lips, amazes me.

"We can't go back," I hazard.

"We can go forward though," he answers quickly, turning towards me and throwing the words back in my face. There's more but immediately, I wish there wasn't. "What I wanted to say to you…what I've tried to say is…I don't suppose…you'd give me another chance?"

Casually, he drops this bombshell, this crash of discordant symphony, into our conversation, compounding the sin by attempting to take hold of my hand. I snatch it away and leap up angrily. Just when I was beginning to believe we were forging a new relationship and all for Daisy's sake!

He rises to his feet, staring at me miserably.

"And this woman back in England, you supposedly love? I suppose she doesn't matter anymore?"

"You don't understand…"

"I understand perfectly!"

"No…you don't…"

"You haven't changed at all!"

His groan at this abuse is loud and clear. "Oh, God, I have changed, Bryony, you've no idea!"

"Hah! As if! Leopard's don't change their spots…"

What he says then, floors me completely.

"But you're the woman I love!"

"What?"

"You're the woman I love… I just couldn't tell you, that was all. Why do you think I've come here? Left the club, missed pre-season training? I had to find you, to tell you how I felt!"

"Of course you don't love me. What a crazy idea…"

"You got it wrong and it seemed easier to play you along than admit how I really felt. You must know you're the reason I'm here. There is no one else; there's never been anyone else…"

At last, thankfully, he runs out of steam, leaving my memory racing back to our last conversation on the topic of his love-life and the certain recollection that I put words into his mouth in assuming the woman he loved was someone, anyone, other than me. I'd no idea he was talking about me!

We've been there, done that and I can't believe he's dredged it all up again. He means it, every word and for the moment, the enormity of what he's just said, temporarily robs me of the ability to speak.

"Would you…I mean, could you…feel that way about me again?"

"Jake I…"

"No! Don't tell me now…think about it at least?"

There's a pause, a miniscule moment stretching into infinity, in which I open my mouth to tell him to put this nonsense right out of his head. But he sounds so sincere, so much, dare I say it, like a man in love, an emotion that's so difficult to associate with Jake. It's a mid-life crisis, a temporary insanity and given his past behaviour, I shouldn't even be giving this a second thought. But then, I think of the effort he's made of late and how easy he's been to be around. Who am I to deny him the chance of trying to turn into a better human being? It's just…well…this is Jake. Jake who is Daisy's father, I remind myself.

I couldn't forgive him for what's gone before. How could I ever forgive him?

Before I can stop him, he steps forward and drops a light kiss on my cheek. His breath is warm on my face and I catch the faint, exotic scent of his aftershave. Traitorously, I feel my body respond. Memories are crowding in on me, like how good we once were together, how once we seemed the perfect fit. Before I discovered the real Jake, I think next, like a drench of ice-cold water. I'm lonely, a typically frustrated, middle-aged woman, I tell myself sternly, and thus a soft target for any vaguely passable bloke, even Jake.

"We'll talk again in a day or two…?" he suggests, looking boyish and uncertain and horribly desirable, even to me, who knows him at his worst. No wonder girls flock round him like bees around the proverbial honey pot. He knows it too but to be fair, that's not his fault.

What do we need to discuss? Do I agree with any of this? My mind is clouded by alcohol and unromantically, for lack of food, my stomach rumbles which Jake affects not to hear. The conversation has run its natural course and we make our way awkwardly, back to the villa, meanwhile avoiding a topic neither of us is presently comfortable with, Jake because he's desperate and I suspect uncertain whether he should have even raised the subject, and me because I'm shocked, confused and resentful he's dumped this in my lap when I wasn't expecting it. I won't be shocked. I'm too old for shocked. He thinks he loves me. I've never loved him. I've been in lust with him which is a totally different kettle of fish. I never did and never have forgiven him for the way we broke up the last time round. But I do feel sorry for him and sorry is a dangerous emotion.

Back at the villa, Edward has supper ready. Max must be eating at the café, Chloe and Milo are yet to return from Agatha's, leaving Daisy free to dominate the table, which thankfully, she does with great aplomb. At least Edward and Simon appear happy enough and what with Father chipping in, here and there, it smoothes over the obvious, that Jake and I are hardly talking, not to anyone else and certainly not to each other.

Half way through the meal, Chloe returns and I can tell by her face, she and Milo have made inroads with Agatha. She's eaten already and takes the opportunity to do what she should have done before, which is to sit and talk to Edward about her plans.

Straight-faced, giving nothing away, Edward listens intently. And yet we all know he's only hiding his marshmallow interior. They argue, the conversation is battered this way and that and to which Father, completely on Chloe's side, can't help adding his four'pennorth. I want to tell him to stop interfering, that it's nothing to do with him, but I don't. After a lengthy while pretending otherwise, as we all knew he would, even Daisy, finally Edward caves in and it appears now, there's nothing to stand in Chloe's way. She springs up and behind Edward's back, she winks at me. She's returning to Anti-Paxos with Milo, first thing in the morning and she has an early start. She's happy, so much is clear, particularly now she's won round both parents.

A short while later, I pack Daisy off to bed, where, despite her protests she's not sleepy yet, she's so worn out with fresh sea air and excitement, she falls to sleep at once. When I return, Father has topped up his wine glass again, the third time to my knowledge and yet he imagines I haven't noticed. If he stays here much longer, he'll kill himself with drink but there again, if I take him back to England, he'll only kill himself with work. He raises his glass towards me. I raise mine back. I can't bear to think how the day might have turned out and am prepared to forgive him anything today, even drinking too much. Edward and Simon take a stroll before turning in, leaving Jake and I to do the washing up, if both studiously avoiding the topic current in our minds.

I've already got enough to think about. I don't need this with Jake.

"I meant it, Bryony," he says at last, unable to help himself. He shakes the soap suds from a plate and passes it to me to dry. He's subdued, earnest, so not the bombastic Jake I know, he's almost, not quite, a stranger to me. Could I learn to love him, if only for Daisy's sake?

"We said we wouldn't talk about it, remember?"

"How could I forget?"

"Don't go getting your hopes up. I can't imagine us back together again."

"Then let your imagination go."

"It isn't that easy, Jake."

I'm only pointing out the obvious but this is Paxos, I remind myself, where easy too easily infiltrates the difficult, catching a body unawares. I'm relieved when it's time to turn in, with its chance to disappear into the sanctuary of my room and where I undress quickly before throwing myself on top of the bed, arms folded beneath my head, to lie staring up at the ceiling, whilst I listen to the house quieten and take on life of its own. I think and ponder, this way and that, stray thoughts rising to the surface or sinking to depths of which I was unaware. But then, as if soft fingers have soothed my brow, my anxieties disappear and my eyes grow heavy and close and I fall to sleep, a calming, refreshing slumber containing an inner certainty, things will turn out right in the end. They will turn out, one way or another, there's nothing so sure of that, and in that nugget of wisdom, I hear my Father's voice.

I'm awoken, not by the dawn, already painting the heavens but by the sense of a growing wonder, as of a new beginning, prompting me to leap out of bed and throw the shutters wide, beguiled by the view waiting to greet me, the world washed anew, a freshly-painted palette of colour, which I see through eyes stripped of pretence. Beyond, the sun glints between the olive trees, turning the leaves a rustling, golden-brown through which the shadows dance. From afar rises a faint murmuring of waves and a faint salt tang of the sea reaches me, intermingling with the birds cooing and roosting in the olive trees.

There's more, too, a sound from beyond the trees, the faint, metallic clink of hoe, on sun-baked soil. It must be Tomas, toiling away on his allotment before it gets too hot to work and I think of the days since I've seen him, that wise old man who knows so much. He went away and now he's returned. Throwing on the first clothes to hand, I hurry downstairs and outside. Bursting into the world of Cassiopeia, as if it's mine and it's only that I've taken a lifetime to discover it. A world of peace and calm, a healing balm to a soul fractured and newly put together again.

And then I remember, what this ridiculous business with Jake has temporarily made me forget, that now I know this villa's secret. It's a matter of moments to pad softly through the warming air, down the terrace steps, to drop onto the path through the olive trees, emerging onto the path circumnavigating Tomas' garden.

He's hoeing up a row of potatoes and straightens up when he sees me, folding his hands over the top of his hoe, on which he rests his chin. His gaze fastens on mine, a man who can't escape the past with which I must confront him. I approach him cautiously, not sure how to start and reminding myself, none of this is the slightest his fault.

"It's good to see you again, Tomas," I begin, inoffensively. "I'm…I'm sorry about your mother. You must feel so sad."

"Ah…"

"Eleni told me...she told me everything and that you'll understand every word I say because you learned both English and German at your mother's knee..."

There's a pause, a second stretching to infinity before he speaks, a husky voice, unused to use.

"Sometime...it expedient to know more than say..."

All that went before has been a pretence, I see so much. I move a little closer, speaking in a hurried whisper, as if I'm worried we might be overheard. "Does no-one know that you're Lillie Drachmann's son? That you're the true owner of Cassiopeia? Your mother made it over to you when you were only a young man. I won't tell anyone, I promise I won't tell anyone!"

It's advisable to assure him of this. His head bows in acknowledgement but then his gaze lifts and he regards me steadily enough. "Only Eleni know. I just old man...old man who looks after garden of Cassiopeia, where Lillie Drachmann knew a little happiness."

He smiles at his words and in his face, for an instance, as if lit from within, I see the young boy he once was, one bearing a striking resemblance to the photograph of a young Lillie Drachmann, shown to me, so dotingly, by Eleni, the only friend Lillie had in the world. The same honest gaze, the same forthright chin. And how difficult it must have been for him during his growing up years, an innocent child, trailed over Europe because his mother could never return to the one place in the world she loved.

"You're Pascal Romano's son...?"

"Or the son of Stefan Drachmann…" he dryly returns. His shoulders lift into a faint shrug. It doesn't matter, the gesture says and I see the truth of this and that it really doesn't matter, only that either father would have loved and been proud of such a son. His eyes burn into mine. "Old history makes houses sad. Too long for Cassiopeia…she want life again! Chase away the sadness of Lillie Drachmann and Pascal Romano and even, Stefan who loved Lillie, too!"

"Is that…is that why you let us stay here?"

He nods and smiles and I understand then, why, over the years, this old man has vetted every single family who wished to come here, mostly turning them down as unsuitable. Cassiopeia is special and so should be the family who stay here. I'm touched, honoured even but perhaps the answer is, we needed Cassiopeia as much as she needed us. Tomas throws down the hoe, looking steadfastly towards his property before holding his arms out wide and his hands, palms upwards. Over the tops of the olive trees, the upper windows of Cassiopeia catch fire in the newly risen sun, like flames dancing on burnished metal. And in my mind's eye, I see once again, the figure of a young girl at the upper window of the villa, looking out over the sea and yearning for her lover, a girl I've vainly looked for time and again. A mirage or a passing fancy, or the ghost of Lillie Drachmann throwing off this mortal coil and returning to Cassiopeia, the one place in the world she loved… A final goodbye, a laying to rest of so much hurt and pain. It's crazy. I'm crazy and yet inside, I believe that this is true.

A figure emerges from between the olive trees, sauntering across the path towards us. Reaching us, he nods an easy greeting to Tomas and then turns back to me. Max, fresh from the arms of Alex, with whom he's spent the night and I think with a pang, my son's grown up.

"You're up and about early, Mum…" he murmurs, shamefaced.

And you thought you'd sneak back in before the house was astir, I muse, though I don't say as much. He has me twisted round his little finger. He glances back, at Cassiopeia and then back to me so that I know what he's going to ask, even before he asks it. He grins widely and then comes out with the craziest, most outlandish notion I've ever heard in my life.

"I love it here, Mum. I love Cassiopeia. Let's stay here forever."

The End

Printed in Great Britain
by Amazon